BEYOND WORLD CLASS

BUILDING CHARACTER, RELATIONSHIPS, AND PROFITS

Alan M. Ross
With Cecil Murphey

Dearborn™
Trade Publishing
A **Kaplan Professional** Company

Senior Acquisitions Editor: Jean Iversen
Senior Managing Editor: Jack Kiburz
Interior Design: Lucy Jenkins
Cover Design: design literate, inc.
Typesetting: Elizabeth Pitts

Library of Congress Cataloging-in-Publication Data

Ross, Alan M.
  Beyond world class : building character, relationships, and profit / by Alan M. Ross, with Cecil Murphey.
    p.   cm.
  ISBN 0-7931-4905-3
  1. Customer relations. 2. Corporate culture. 3. Human capital. 4. Success in business. I. Murphey, Cecil B. II. Title.
  HF5415.5 .R67 2002
  658.8'12—dc21
                                                    2001003599

PRAISE FOR *BEYOND WORLD CLASS: BUILDING CHARACTER, RELATIONSHIPS, AND PROFITS*

"*Beyond World Class* is an easy and excellent book to read. Alan Ross and Cec Murphey have done a great job identifying the meaning of building a company around covenantal relationships. All of us want to lead a company beyond profits and numbers to truly have a positive impact on the people (employees, customers, and suppliers) along the way. I found the book to be informative, challenging, and inspired, and one I will reread from time to time. My goal is to move our company beyond world class with the same passion this book represents."

—Dwight Armstrong, Ph.D., President, COO, Akey, Inc.

"Alan Ross superbly communicates to CEOs. He has been where we are and is uniquely qualified to help corporate leaders take the next crucial step in building their firms. In *Beyond World Class*, Alan Ross shows us how to understand and establish covenantal relationships in a workplace of broken promises. In a full employment economy, we are shown how to build trust for high employee retention. In a financial market based on quarterly numbers, he shares with us how to build long-term businesses. This is a must-read for CEOs who want to swim upstream against the latest marketplace fads."

—Kent Humphreys, American Health Diagnostics

"*Beyond World Class* shows how one can successfully create tremendous value that doesn't show up on the balance sheet in the form of an intangible asset. Most Wall Street analysts recognize the value of brand equity, market share, and other components as this type of asset. Alan Ross shows how relationships with our employees and customers can create a culture that is invaluable and can sustain a company through all kinds of business climates. When you have created this type of corporate culture, you have become the employer or supplier of choice."

—William J. Bolthouse, President, Wm. Bolthouse Farms, Inc.

"This book conveys extraordinary insights and experiences about the building blocks and quality elements forming the inner life of a corporation and its staff, and how these will impact the company's performance. It provides a doorway to discover with new depth how to impact the world and can become the start of a journey toward lasting success in its deepest sense—true servanthood."

—J. Gunnar Olson, Chairman and Founder, International Christian Chamber of Commerce

"The mission of the U.S. Merchant Marine Academy is to educate and graduate mariners and leaders for honorable service to our nation. The principles of *Beyond World Class* will be valuable for the leadership education of our midshipmen and are also useful for the professional growth of the academy's faculty, staff, and coaches. We look forward to placing several copies in the ethics and leadership area of the academy library."

—Rear Admiral Joe Steward, Superintendent, U.S. Merchant Marine Academy

"*Beyond World Class* is bold in that it exposes the shortsightedness of traditional quarter-to-quarter management that so many large companies operate under today. It exposes flaws in such thinking and demonstrates how real value gets created in today's dynamic corporations. Ross challenges the paradigm that truth is relative and helps the reader see that truth is absolute in every business situation. He's been able to demonstrate with practical examples from real-life companies how leaders who deal only in their absolute truths are the most successful."

—Larry G. Walker, Managing Director, Global Financial Industry Strategy, EDS

"Serving the customer is a theme of many books, but this one takes it a step further. Alan Ross writes about serving the customer through new solutions to their problems and through covenantal relationships, which involves building a character culture. He has some great insights into serving and developing such a culture. This book is a timely reminder with true wisdom."

—Stanley Vermeer, President, The Barzillai Foundation

"This book aspires to lift your thinking above the currently accepted business level and take you off the beaten track into new territory for the development of your business. If you want to have your traditional business practice confirmed, then put this book down. If you want to be challenged to achieve new heights, then reading this book is time well spent."

—Peter J. Briscoe, President, Europartners

"Here is a business book with great ideas—compelling, principle-based, proven, and effective. What you won't find here are this month's fads (and next month's flops)! You and I need to go beyond world class to transform our companies, and this book shows us how."

—John D. Beckett, CEO/President, R.W. Beckett Corporation, and Author of *Loving Monday: Succeeding in Business without Selling Your Soul*

"I love the stories! They are real people in real situations doing real things. *Beyond World Class* is one of the few books where leadership theory climbs in the trenches and slugs it out with life. It is not just the rubber meets the road. It's squealing tires and blue smoke on hot pavement. It's about making money, building businesses, and loving people—not pie in the sky, but real lives on the ground. Get it, do it, and change your business. Change your life."

—Brian Ray, President/CEO, Crossroads Career Network

"Employees across North America told us in our most recent survey the most important part of their job is to be trusted to do it well and make a difference in the company. Alan Ross tells how you can do just that with covenant relationships with all stakeholders. The successful companies are those that keep the best people and the best customers. *Beyond World Class* shares with you the 'how to'!"

—Jim Reese, CEO, Randstad North America

"Wow! What a powerful book of teachings and examples of biblical principles. Everyone should follow these beyond world class directions. Our Lord would say, 'Well done my faithful servant.'"

—Jim Dismore, Chairman/CEO/President, Ultimate Support Systems, Inc.

"Alan Ross is focused on helping leaders involved with larger companies enhance their efforts to make a positive impact through their influence in the marketplace."

—Jim Moye, President/CEO, Moye Financial Associates, Inc.

DEDICATION

I am grateful to our staff at Corporate Development Institute (CDI), especially to Phyllis Rice, my executive assistant, and Tony Collins, my partner, both of whom have challenged me to live and lead a beyond-world-class life; to the many friends in the marketplace, who have allowed me to hone my craft by opening their hearts and the doors of their companies; to the members and leaders of Fellowship of Companies for Christ International (FCCI) who encouraged me to develop this vision while serving as their leader; and to my friend and coauthor Cecil Murphey, who brings the best out in all he touches.

Most important is my thanks to my wife Sara and to our sons Patrick and Michael—my greatest sources of joy, delight, and encouragement. They are my greatest sponsors. Finally, I am eternally grateful to God for faithfully guiding the steps of my life, showing me the vision of beyond world class, and encouraging me to "take a leap of faith."

CONTENTS

CHAPTER ONE

A BUSINESS PARABLE

Everyone in the art world knew the work of Zach, who was a master painter. Even his rivals bought his work for its beauty and craft. One day, a group of eight art students came to his studio and said, "You paint masterpieces, master Zach. Would you teach us how to paint like you?"

"Yes, I will do that," he answered. "But you must do what I ask you to do." He handed each of them a large canvas, exactly the same size as the one he was working on. "Here are your brushes," Zach said as he passed them out.

Among the small group were three students of outstanding talent. Two were right-handed and one left-handed. The first right-handed man reached out with his right hand to take the set of brushes.

"Yes, that is correct," Zach said.

Next was the left-handed man and, as was his nature, he extended his left hand.

"No! No! You must reach out with your right hand and take them, as the man in front of you did," Zach commanded.

"But I'm not right-handed."

"What do I care about that?" Zach asked. "You will do it the way I say to do it. You must follow my technique exactly—from the taking of the brush into your hand until you put away your paints."

The second man shrugged and did as he was told.

The third student, broad and tall, had extremely large hands. Zach handed him the brushes, which were quite small. "They are small and difficult to hold," the student complained.

"What do I care about that?" Zach again answered.

Next, Zach gave each man a palette—and made certain they held it exactly as he held his. "You will start by mixing red and blue." He demonstrated and added the slightest touch of white and a tiny dab of ochre. When he finished, on the pallette was an exquisite shade of purple—the finest, most delicate color anyone had seen.

The students marveled over the color.

"Now that you have watched me do this, you do exactly what I did."

Each student followed Zach's instructions exactly. They all ended up with purple—not quite as delicate looking, but a more beautiful shade than any one of them had created before.

Zach arched a brow as he watched the clumsy left-handed, would-be painter. The student dropped the brush twice because he had trouble stirring with his right hand. The student with large hands had trouble painting the delicate lines with a tiny brush, but he kept on. Zach worked patiently with him, however, and even he completed the task.

None of their work looked as good as the master's, but they admitted they had improved.

"Now you must follow each brush stroke that I make as I paint a sunset," Zach requested.

Each student did exactly as the master did. Stroke for stroke the students followed him.

"Ahhh," they said each time the master mixed a new color. By the end of the day, Zach had created a masterpiece of brilliant hues and tones beyond anything any of them had ever seen.

Zach looked around for the first time since he had begun to paint. All eight students had completed their work, even the left-handed one, whose work he scrutinized first. "Sir, I suggest that you just choose another profession. Painting is definitely not for you."

Then one by one, he examined the other seven. He nodded or smiled, and offered such words as, "Yes, this is good—that is, it is good for your first try." After he had looked at every painting, he requested, "Come back tomorrow. You will do the same thing again and each day after that. You will learn a little bit more of my technique and you will get better. You will get to the point where you can paint as well as I can, although," he chuckled, "perhaps not as good as I do."

While everyone had painted the same sunset, only Zach had created a masterpiece.

The eight students left the room, all with downcast faces and discouraged hearts. Each day they returned and continued to mimic the master painter. None of the students became great painters; all of them became great imitators.

Across the hallway from Zach, a man named Ramos had a studio and he was also an outstanding painter. After a few months, the same group of eight aspiring artists, who had been disappointed with Zach, went to him.

"You are a master painter, sir," one of them said, "and we wish to learn to paint. Will you teach us?"

Ramos walked up to the first student and said, "Close your eyes."

The student obeyed.

"Now I want you to see the picture that you've been destined to paint."

"Destined? Uh, but . . . but . . ."

"Shh. Close your eyes, visualize, and wait."

No one made a sound for several minutes. Then the first man opened his eyes. "I saw it! I saw it!"

"What did you see?" asked Ramos.

"A little girl. I saw her face quite close. It was tilted slightly to the left. I'm not sure if she was smiling or crying, but a tear had begun to slip from the corner of her eye."

"Ah, yes, yes, that is the picture you were destined to paint. Now let me see your hands." The student held out his hands. Ramos stared at them and then lightly ran his fingertips over the man's palms. "What delicate hands. You have chosen well, obviously, because you have the kind of hands that would paint a portrait. For portraits, it's probably best to use these paints with small brushes." He handed him a small brush. "Hold it and close your eyes. How does the brush feel?"

The student held the brush and a smile emerged.

"Yes, that is right. Now here is what I want you to do." Ramos pointed to large jars of paint. "Keep your eyes closed until you picture the little girl's face and can focus on that single tear. Examine its color closely. Now you will mix these paints until you have the exact color you desire. It may take you hours perhaps, but you must continue until the color on your palette is the color you saw in your vision. Do you understand?"

The student nodded.

"Excellent. After you have mixed your perfect color, then you must paint the tear. When you have done that, the rest of the picture will come automatically and you will finish it."

The student followed Ramos's instructions and carefully began to mix the paints.

Next, the teacher went to the second student and said, "I want you to see the picture that you've been destined to paint."

After a few minutes, the student said, "I see a vista. It's a landscape with a waterfall and a rainbow."

"Excellent," said the teacher. "Now let me see your hands."

The student was the tall, broad-shouldered man with large, muscular hands. After Ramos examined them, he said, "Yes, this is right. It is good, because obviously you have chosen a picture that demands big hands. It would be difficult for you to paint that scene with the tools the other student is using."

Ramos handed the second student watercolors and told him to exercise the same care in mixing his colors. "Your colors should be vibrant. Focus on the brightest color of the rainbow. Close your eyes and keep them closed until you see it again."

"Yes, I see it."

"Excellent. Start with that color and when you have mixed and painted it, the rest will come."

One by one, Ramos spoke with each of the eight students. Each time, he started by saying, "I want you to see the picture that you've been destined to paint."

To the left-handed student, he said, "Don't try to paint with your right hand. You must paint your picture with the hand that is most natural to you."

Soon all eight students were absorbed in their individual works. When finished, each painting was different and yet each was a masterpiece, and the others admired it. The students looked around to thank the teacher, but the teacher was gone.

"He has taught us that we don't need him," said the student with large hands. "He showed us the way, but it was our picture to paint, not his."

"If he had stayed and taken us step by step through the process," said the left-handed man, "it would still have been his painting, made with our hands, but still his."

In this parable, each of the young men painted his own masterpiece because Ramos had allowed and encouraged them to follow their basic nature and approach to the canvas. Each one produced a different picture, but all were excellent.

That's how I see success in business. Too many books, lectures, and seminars try to make every entrepreneur think and act a certain way. If we don't have our Day Timers list of A, B, and C things to do, we don't know how to function.

That's not my purpose in writing this book. My vision, as demonstrated in the story, is that each of you has your own abilities and need only to be shown the way to create a masterpiece. Your business ventures aren't my masterpiece. I don't want to teach you or anyone else to do things my way. You can't work the way I do, and I'm not asking you to follow seven specific steps to achieve a masterpiece.

I want you to discover your unique method of working. If you do it your way, you'll create your own work of art—and it will be *yours!* I will have encouraged you and offered help along the way, but the final canvas will be your creation.

Consider the implications of this parable in real life. What would happen if the CEO in a large company said, "I want you to visualize the role you have been destined to fulfill in this company"?

Can you imagine what would happen in the business community if each CEO said such words to vice presidents, managers, coordinators, and every employee down to the custodial staff?

The question may sound as if it invites chaos—everyone going in different directions and each having his or her own vision. But guess what? That's how business operates today. However, because companies print mission statements, policies, and slogans, they assume everyone is marching forward together and at the same pace. That perception is wrong.

We all have our own agendas, dreams, desires, visions, and hopes. Probably none of us knows all of the pulsating forces in our own lives. The most powerful ones may be driving us on an unconscious level, and we receive little help because no one else knows what they are, and we have little incentive to share them. Few of us have the opportunity to close our eyes and clearly envision those dreams and then work toward fulfilling them.

My parable is really about personal destiny.

If you follow your personal destiny in cooperation with others, you'll discover what I mean when I refer to companies that are "beyond world class." Like Ramos, the organization itself becomes the great master teacher. Students will keep coming back, and they also will bring others. The company will expand. Unfortunately, though, we have too many Zachs at the heads of companies today, and the situation worsens because we keep hiring or promoting them. What we need are more Ramoses.

In this book I want to show you how to learn and follow the Ramos pattern. Who knows? Maybe you will not only paint your own masterpiece, but also become a person to whom others will come to learn.

It is possible.

CHAPTER TWO

BECOMING A BEYOND-
WORLD-CLASS COMPANY

I believe in world-class companies. I believe more strongly in companies that are beyond world class. I've been part of both kinds.

For someone to call their company "world class" may seem boastful. To call it "beyond world class" sounds arrogant. *World class* refers to financially strong companies that produce quality products. That's good—it's just not good enough.

World class sets high standards. Such companies develop strategies that improve quality, lower costs, meet or exceed customer expectations, and create long-term shareholder value. This effectively produces financial rewards that shareholders expect in today's highly competitive world.

That's better—but it's not yet good enough.

Beyond-world-class companies model something far better than mere financial returns. Those returns become a by-product of a more significant component of a business—a component that is quickly vanishing in a world absorbed with consumption and short-term rewards. I want all members of an organization to know clearly the difference in their beyond-world-class company, and to experience the difference daily.

I want customers and suppliers to understand that they are part of something very special, being challenged themselves to live for a "higher calling" than mere survival or financial success.

That concept begins with individual leaders who commit themselves to those beyond-world-class principles by modeling and teaching them as they lead with excellence.

THE POWER OF THE COVENANT

A beyond-world-class company strives for world-class results, but instead of emphasizing financial results, a beyond-world-class company teaches its leaders to covenant customers, suppliers, and employees. *It is possible to create a world-class company without addressing this key component; it is impossible to get beyond-world-class status without experiencing the incredible power of a covenant relationship.*

Before we can truly grasp the principles that lead to a beyond-world-class company, we must clearly understand this concept of covenant relationships. As you'll read throughout this book, I use the word *covenant* often because it's a vital ingredient of a beyond-world-class company.

I contrast covenants with contracts and agreements. *Contract principles*—used in most management or leadership practices—create and define expectations and outcomes by the terms of the contract, such as the consequences of not living up to the stipulations of the contract. Although such words may sound good, they restrict the conditions and the results.

Covenants release; contracts bind. Covenants ask "What is possible?" while contracts state "This is permissible." Covenantal agreements enable people to ask "What if . . . ?" and unleash collective brilliance and individual excellence. The covenant principle means acting in the best interest of others while aligning with the vision and mission of the company. That includes employees, customers, and suppliers. We covenant with our employees by setting a high standard of opportunity, excellence, and responsibility, and thereby release them to reach their fullest potential and not limit themselves to their contractual conditions.

By contrast, most companies call themselves successful or world class based on four performance indicators:

1. *Profitability.* Every company has to make money to stay in business. Today, the term *values-based leadership* essentially starts with profitability.

2. *Shareholder value.* As profits rise, so does the stock value. Long-term shareholder value is an important indicator of the health and vitality of a company.

3. *Market position.* Measured in market shares, these are the indicators of how well a company can maximize the first two indicators. It's a highly competitive issue of achieving market dominance.

4. *Return on assets/investments/sales.* These measure the results that management achieves in relation to the application of resources.

These are high-order results for beyond-world-class companies, right?

Wrong!

When we talk about *beyond* world class, we mean something quite different. Profitability, shareholder value, market share, and return on assets aren't high-level items. If a company operates by the principles of beyond world class, it'll achieve significant results as measured by these financial indicators, but the results are the by-product of a much greater result. Too often financial success is fleeting in the corporate world. Even a large corporation that is at the top one year can experience a major fall the next. Reading the financial news regularly points out that obvious fact.

Beyond-world-class companies consider those four indicators low-order results. They're important and we can't push them aside, but they're not part of the *intrinsic* value of the employees, customers, or the suppliers that we work with. We believe those four results are the easy part. If all we had to do were to make a company profitable, to meet impressive financial objectives, then our job would be quite easily defined and made much simpler.

What's difficult—and this is what makes a company part of beyond world class—is to take those commonly accepted goals and turn them upside down. What many have used to measure success and top-priority achievements within their organizations, we accept as an outcome of the higher-level results.

So what do we consider higher-level results?

1. *We create intrinsic value by bringing out the very best in our employees, customers, and suppliers.* Not only do we value them—they *know* they're valued for the right reasons. We have high-level expectations for performance, but we also have important expectations of leaders to integrate performance with relationships.

2. *We work for long-term employee retention.* More than just avoiding turnover, those employees express high levels of job satisfaction, which, of course, make them want to stay with the company.

3. *We maintain a high-retention rate of suppliers.* We begin by trying to pick the best suppliers. They're the ones who go out of their way to offer the best service. (Our surveys also show that these suppliers consider *us* the best companies to work with. They know, for instance, that when we give our word, we keep it.)

4. *We retain the best customers.* Our customers become satisfied so they readily enter into loyal, long-term relationships with us. As we explain later, we become covenantal partners.

5. *We strive to be long-term winners.* We don't have to be number one, but we're always in the lead by constantly learning how to improve everything we do. We survive changes in our particular field, our leadership and our organizations are secure, and people know they can depend on us. We are the companies that people look to for long-term solutions and lasting value.

When we have these high-order priorities working, we prosper and become highly profitable. But even more important, we become highly respected organizations and, for beyond-world-class companies, the values such as respect, loyalty, and trust take precedence over profit.

Despite the vagaries of the economy, the ups and downs in the marketplace, and an increasingly difficult world to compete in, beyond-world-class companies remain strong and grow. In the following chapters, you'll learn what we do to make ourselves beyond world class, but I can sum it up in one sentence: *We prosper over time because we hold and maintain the right values.* We emphasize internal values and commitments, and they remain foremost in our thinking. The changes that take place *externally* don't overwhelm, threaten, or change us. We're prepared for whatever comes and we're always ready to adapt, to transform ourselves, even to reinvent ourselves when necessary.

A DISTINCT DIFFERENCE

Whenever I speak to leaders about becoming beyond world class, they commonly ask the four questions that follow.

1. Are Beyond-World-Class Principles Mutually Exclusive from Other Business Models?

The answer is yes. Several management MBA programs urge students to use values in their professions. Some universities teach and speak of "value added" business. The trouble is that no matter what terms are used in the curriculum, their focus is still kept in the wrong place. They emphasize and urge their students to aim for low-order results such as profitability, shareholder value, and market-share dominance.

It is often taught that the objective of leadership is to maximize those profits and the results that go with them, so the focus is on the outcome in the short run, rather than the process in the long run. The reality is that if we retain the best customers, employees, and suppliers while we become a "solutions provider," the results are profitability and success. Others tend to measure success by profit-and-loss statements or ratings. We accept success as the proven outcome of hard work.

2. Is It Difficult to Become a Beyond-World-Class Company?

Although it's not difficult to achieve, it's often difficult to start. It may be impossible for some organizations to turn that concept upside down, because they have made profitability their god and the one acceptable mark of their success.

It's not easy to become a beyond-world-class company—and it's never a static situation but one of constant improvement and refinement. However, it can be done! In fact, we also can assure you that the change can start almost anywhere within the organization. The loading dock foreman could be the first to begin to transform that company into one that is beyond world class.

For example, if that foreman applied the principles and influenced ten others, the beyond-world-class concepts would operate—not fully, but they would work. If a hundred people caught the vision and made the simple commitments of beyond world class, together they could influence and eventually change the entire company.

The worst, and least effective, way for beyond world class to come into an organization is when the CEO accepts the principles but becomes the only one committed to them, or views the principles as just another method or system to try. It won't permeate the company. Only when CEOs and other leaders make transformational changes in their own thinking, and are willing to influence others to make the same kind of changes, can this happen. Those who seek to implement the principles must themselves first be committed to them. CEOs or middle managers can't tell others how to do it, but rather they need to put the principles into action themselves.

3. Will the Change to a Beyond-World-Class Company Be Worth It?

Yes! I have personally applied these principles in more than a hundred companies. Whenever leaders have lived by these principles, those companies produced extremely well in the way people judge successful companies. They've increased in profitability, shareholder value, and market-share dominance. But more important, we have also seen high-order results. That is, employees, suppliers, and customers are valued and they remain loyal.

In more than 100 instances, we worked with or created organizations that were growing and learning companies, and they all achieved the intrinsic high-order results. When we put the priorities in the right order, we achieved our beyond-world-class goals *and* achieved high profits.

We had a lot of fun and satisfaction in bringing that about. The one sad fact—and I want to be open about this—is that some of those beyond-world-class companies didn't continue. When the significant change agents left, those who followed didn't walk in their footsteps. They couldn't, because they didn't have the same vision as their predecessors.

That leads me to another principle of beyond world class— we have to teach the next generation, those who follow the present workers and leaders.

"That's impossible," one manager complained. "We have such a high turnover of employees. Why, it would be like training people to work for our competitors."

"That's just the point," I responded. "Once you become beyond world class, you won't have that high attrition rate. You'll also end up retraining your competitors' people." I wanted him to realize that companies that work with beyond-world-class principles retain their people, and they don't stop there. They become the mentors and trainers for those that follow them. That's a high-yield, low-cost benefit.

That means that one of the clearest characteristics of a beyond-world-class company is the current leadership's commitment to prepare, mentor, and empower the next generation of leadership. I like to think of it as a relay race where the present leaders circle the track. They run their best, and spectators can see their efforts to forge ahead. Those leaders also know that when they finish their lap, they'll pass on the baton to the next person in line. In this relay, participants are responsible to run their portion the best they can; they know they aren't finished until they pass on the baton—but only to the next person in line. They have no responsibility for the third person or the last person. The best they can do is to make sure it's a great hand-off to the right person.

If we do it well, we may find that the race isn't a relay around the same track but more like a marathon. When the leaders hand on the baton, they leave the stadium. By the successful handing over, the true power of the beyond-world-class company takes hold. New runners discover tracks their predecessors never considered, and they end up charting an entirely new course.

4. How Do We Change to Beyond World Class?

This change comes about by following three transforming strategies. I can explain these principles best by presenting the J. Smith Lanier (JSL) Company—one of the largest, fastest-growing, private and commercial insurance brokerage firms in the country—as a beyond-world-class model. They already had a long history of success when we began to work with them in 1997.

STRATEGIC PRINCIPLES

Before we met with JSL, the CEO, J. Smith Lanier, had already committed to making his company one with intrinsic values that was beyond world class. After he had developed a successful business, Smith realized that he was getting older and needed to prepare himself to pass on the baton. That's the major reason he brought in Corporate Development Institute (CDI).

Together, we established three strategic principles that would guide the company through the transition.

1. Be Customer Focused

The first principle was to serve customers. We challenged leadership to define their client base, the "sweet spot" of the market where they were most likely to be successful—and they could define it by focusing on those customers with whom they had been consistently successful in the past.

We also asked them to covenant with their customers, which we'll explain in the next chapter. The power of the customer covenant is transformational to a company because, by its very nature, the covenant requires a complete shift in focus.

We challenged them to understand customers at a completely different level. Rather than ask their customers "What can we do to serve you?" which is critically important but not necessarily transformational, we taught them how to ask their customers an even more important question, "How can we help you better serve your customers and succeed in your industry?"

2. Distinguish between External and Internal Customers

External customers buy our products or services. But many organizations fail to focus on their internal customers—those who work within the organization but don't come into contact with the final customer-client. Instead, they serve somebody who produces something for the external customer.

For example, let's say I'm in policy management. After a client says yes, my job description states that I review their policy and coverage. I don't meet the people taking out the coverage, but I do my work on behalf of the client-services team. Once I've finished, the client-services team presents my work to the customer. At no point am I visible to the buyers. However, even if the buyers don't see me, I still need to serve my client-services team and to understand that I'm part of a team that serves the ultimate client. If I don't know the client needs, such as the timing and the specific issues that the client-services team deals with, I won't serve them. If I don't serve that team, ultimately, they can't serve the clients. When the client-services team is valued and served—as an internal customer, I want to and am able to serve the external clients.

JSL management fervently embraced the concept of internal customers, because their significant problems were between departments. It made sense that changing the nature of the relationship between people in those departments would energize them to solve problems. The best result, however, was the way the employees grasped the concept. Once it became a part of their culture, the way they worked together was changed forever.

They made serving their internal customers a high priority, and that attitude, once put into practice, revolutionized their thinking. You can guess what happened. Their sales and profitability shot up dramatically. All because they turned their focus on serving customers—*all* their customers.

This isn't a new concept in the marketplace—the information has been around since the early 1980s—but it stays new until a company actually puts the concept into operation, as JSL did. Had anyone asked before we began to work with them in 1997, the people at JSL would have said, "We're the most customer-service focused company in the industry, and that's why we're so successful." The problem is, they didn't understand the power of covenant in serving their customers.

After they clearly understood their customer base and the future needs of their customers, we encouraged them to take the next step and establish covenant relationships with them. We urged them to build an organization that always seeks to do what is in the best interest of the customer in alignment with the vision, purpose, and guiding principles of the J. Smith Lanier Company.

"Be prepared," we warned them. "This step into covenant relationships will probably be the most difficult for you to implement. The concept is based on understanding clearly your own vision, mission, and guiding principles and not very many companies truly know that." While most companies have taken up the vision or mission mantra of the 1980s and 1990s, few of them understand and apply it. Too often the vision and mission statements become just statements or plaques on the wall. They're meant to be the lifeblood of the company, like the stars that guided sailors of old. If the position of the stars was ever changing like many visions, missions, or guiding principles, how could anyone navigate?

To their credit, JSL adapted with speed and excellence to this new way of relating to customers internally and externally. By taking that step, it also pushed them to rethink all the relationships within their organization. Everyone at JSL didn't readily accept what we taught, no matter how hard we tried. Some simply resisted, and others just didn't see that it was worth doing. A few employees left during that time, which was probably a wise decision, because they would have had a difficult time adjusting to these new principles.

Those who did stay, however, and understood the power of covenant relationships, leapfrogged the whole company forward. The corporate leaders modeled the principles we wanted to teach, so it wasn't hard for most people to understand what they saw in someone else.

"You've lost a generation," we told them. "The next handoff isn't ready." They understood and allowed us to prepare for that handoff. Within two years, the next generation was ready to grab the baton. Then J. Smith Lanier and the old leaders did the hardest part—they left the stadium. Now the next baton carriers could begin to chart a new course for the company—all the while aligning it with the vision, mission, and guiding principles. That handing over revolutionized the company.

3. Seek Continuous Solutions Development

JSL had to reinvent itself. The company did that by learning to seek and solve potential problems before they could impact their commitment to excellence. "We must continuously provide high-order solutions both internally and externally," they said. "And that process must involve serving customers."

They changed their approach from *meeting* problems and making decisions, to *anticipating* problems. We helped them develop a program, called it "Fortress 2000," and subtitled it, "Building a Fortress around Your Customers."

We knew that JSL had changed when one of their top leaders said to a customer, "In the past, we saw our job as reviewing your policies and seeing if we could produce a better one for your protection. Now, our job is to build a fortress around you— a risk-management fortress—and keep you protected from any attacks or negative developments."

"Risk-management fortress? What's that?" the customer immediately asked.

"We're going to build a fortress around you to make sure that you don't take unnecessary insurance or liability risks. If you have risk problems, we want to work with you in every area to eliminate them at the lowest possible cost so you can employ your resources to better serve your customers. We manage the risks so you can build your business."

This approach once again impacted the company. The lower-order results are better than they've ever been with record profits and asset utilization. They don't lose good people to the competition. The average turnover rate in that industry is about 10 percent a year. The turnover rate at JSL in 1999 was *1 percent.* This fact is so well known that they have a list of people wanting to come work for them. They get to select the best employees because they have higher-quality applicants to choose from. Even their industry competitors say, sometimes grudgingly, "They're the best."

Here are a few additional reasons JSL is the best:

- They provide opportunities for advancement through a powerful employee-development program.

- They don't lose customers because someone offers to undersell. In fact, one JSL competitor remarked, "It's difficult to take away a J. Smith Lanier client."

- Suppliers of the products they broker work harder in partnering with JSL to create solutions for those clients, because these suppliers have come to recognize their value and the commitment they have to the covenant with customers. JSL has become their internal customer. By serving them covenantally, they serve JSL customers.

To illustrate this last point, at one suppliers' meeting held at JSL, they asked, "What can we do to serve you better?"

"Just by asking us that question you've done more than any of the other companies we do business with," one supplier replied.

"That's right. Nobody ever really cares. What they ask us is, 'What can you do to serve *our* customers better?' That's what we want to do, but nobody ever came to us before and asked, 'What can *we* do to serve you better?'"

Something else happens in this kind of relationship that goes beyond buying and selling. The suppliers eagerly go the extra mile on behalf of JSL customers.

As we've continued to work with JSL, we've been aware of an invisible line that links the company with their employees and their suppliers and clients. They're all part of it, and most of them realize it. That makes them a beyond-world-class company.

Following these three strategic principles was not as easy as it seemed, but JSL went through the process we gave them. Just going through the steps changed their business approach and outlook. In doing so, they also became more financially successful—but that had not been their primary goal.

THE LEGACY

Earlier I spoke of J. Smith Lanier's concern about passing on the torch to the next generation. I want to tell you about that event. In January 1998, I attended and spoke at their annual meeting. They had already completed the first phases of the transformation, and I congratulated them and encouraged them to keep on.

When my speech ended, I asked J. Smith Lanier and his partner, COO, Billy Parr, Jr., to stand in front of the entire company. Then I called Gaines Lanier, the new CEO, and Gary Ivey, the new COO, to come forward.

I turned toward the audience, "You are about to watch the handoff. The responsibility now rests with the generation in this room. Your job is to make sure that the next handoff is even smoother. It will be harder because you'll be a lot bigger. You will have more people, more opportunities, and a greater responsibility to manage even more resources. You will encounter new, complicated problems because your industry is going through a lot of change. You are preparing for your task to make those problems easier."

We brought in a flaming Olympic torch and handed it to the current CEO and COO, who held it together. It was one of those rare human moments that defy explanation. All of us knew instinctively that it was a powerful event in the history of the company. We had just passed on the higher-order values of JSL to the next generation.

The two older men handed over the torch. Eyes filled with tears, some clapped, and a few shouted.

As of this writing, we're preparing for the next generation of leaders. The JSL leaders have five to seven years to identify, mentor, and develop them.

By the way, the company is no longer the same as it was when they passed the torch in 1998. Within three years, it has already doubled in size. And with each phase of growth, along comes the low-level result—higher profitability. If they continue, they'll double within the next three years. If they hold to the values, they'll truly stand high among beyond-world-class companies.

But what about a larger company where the name on the CEO's office door isn't the name of the company? Or what about a company that finds itself in a ditch, or that flounders financially with little sense of direction? Does beyond world class work there too? Can these principles transform a company that has consistently violated most of them?

Let's find out.

CHAPTER THREE

STRATEGY TOWARD BEYOND WORLD CLASS

They said a turnaround couldn't happen, but it did—and in only 18 months. Sklar Pepplar Furniture, a Canadian manufacturer, hired me in 1991 because they were in deep trouble. In Canada they call it CCAA; in the United States it is Chapter 11.

Somehow, my company, North American Mercantile, was able to pull the company back from the edge of the abyss. Sklar Pepplar would survive—but survival wasn't enough. Where would they go from there?

Before I answer, I want to provide a little background. Sklar Pepplar was a merger of two older, established furniture makers. For half a century, Sklar Furniture had been one of the largest and most recognized Canadian furniture manufacturers before merging with Pepplar Brothers Furniture, another well-known and highly respected company.

Prior to the merger, both had been successful. For many years after the merger, the Sklar Pepplar Furniture Company continued to grow and prosper as one of Canada's premier furniture manufacturers. Then in the mid 1980s, the leveraged buyout phenomenon forced the Sklar family to sell out. It was a takeover based on the potential value of the stock, not the value the families had placed on the business for more than 40 years.

From the beginning of the new leadership, things began to turn bad. The fast tracking of the North American Free Trade Agreement (NAFTA) changed things for the worse, and the Canadian dollar soared to a near all-time high. These two events combined to create huge and growing losses, until they were forced into CCAA. For tax reasons, I wasn't able to take the title of president because I was really working on behalf of our American company, where I was president and CEO. North American Mercantile had the turnaround responsibility at Sklar Pepplar. As executive vice president, it was my job to right a sinking ship.

I put together a hard-working team, all of whom had been in positions of leadership at Sklar before I arrived. With their help and a loyal base of Canadian retailers, we managed to stop the slide and finally knew we wouldn't have to close Sklar Pepplar's doors. Just to hang on and stay in business wasn't enough, though.

As the new leader, my first task was to seek out Lou Sklar, former chairman and the last family member in the company. I sat with Lou for hours and listened as he shared the early years, the growth years, and finally the hostile takeover.

"They had no heart for the business," he said wistfully. "I knew it was a matter of time before they killed it. We always valued the people and they seemed to value only the money."

Lou was right.

A COMMITMENT TO EXCELLENCE

"What do we have to do to re-establish ourselves as the best in Canada?" I asked my leadership team. I think they were surprised by my declared intent not merely to survive but to succeed.

As we wrestled with that question, we first had to admit one of the problems: We had not learned how to serve our customers *with excellence*. We were as good as any other company, but that wasn't enough. Before considering that question, we already had decided to become a beyond-world-class company, so being as good as another manufacturer meant setting the standard too low. If we were to be the best Canadian supplier, we also had to compete in a global arena.

We also decided to establish *covenant relationships*—though none of us fully understood exactly what was meant by that phrase or how to make such relationships work. This may sound like an odd term, so one way to say it is that we decided to make ethics part of the foundation. We wanted to be people of our word. For instance, whatever we promised, we would deliver— and do it with excellence.

"So where do we start?" the board asked. We then decided that, as a first step, we needed to focus on our customers—the retailers. We talked to them and did costly surveys. We couldn't make any changes until we had all the information and it had to come from them. We needed to know what changes were taking place in our customers' businesses. Things were changing all across the country. Before we made our decisions, we needed a better base of understanding.

We began with those who had been Sklar Pepplar customers the longest. We chose Eaton's—a large Canadian department store chain. Their relationship with Sklar went back 50 years, and they stayed with us and bought from us, although we had lost sales volume with them. For many years, we had been their number one furniture supplier. Now we had dropped to a number too low to matter. American companies had taken over the floor space that Sklar Pepplar once took for granted.

"What do your customers want from you?" we asked the executives at Eaton's. We went beyond the furniture buyers to the corporate management and the key leadership. Like all department stores, Eaton's was going through its own share of turmoil as a result of changes in the marketplace. Canadians surged across the border to buy goods from American retailers because their value was much higher.

Once they understood our questions—that we were asking about their customers—a dialogue began that eventually led to a partnership commitment between Eaton's and Sklar Pepplar to recapture the loyalty and sales dollar of the Canadian furniture consumer.

But first, we had a lot to learn.

"You're too expensive for the marketplace," we heard most often. "The Americans have come in with lower-priced products, and believe it or not, they offer equal quality. Because we rely most heavily on Canadian suppliers, we have been hit much harder than our competition. Our loyalty to Sklar Pepplar has cost us dearly."

"Your designs are old-fashioned," we heard almost as often. "Americans are more high-fashion oriented. We didn't think Canadians would like that, but we went along with the Americans and, to our amazement, learned that our customers like what they produce. We are trying to adjust our floors to represent what consumers want today and you still carry what they wanted years ago."

"They ship our orders quickly," was the third most frequent response. One executive explained, "You don't understand just-in-time inventory management. We order from Sklar Pepplar and it takes 12 weeks. We order from an American company and it is shipped to us in 2 weeks. This cuts our service time to customers on special orders by 8 weeks. It also allows us to carry far less inventory than we've had to carry from you. We turn our inventory three times faster than we did when you were our number one supplier."

We received a few other responses, but those three came up every time we asked. Now we knew their needs. The problem was identified but even Eaton's did not believe we could come up with a significant solution.

We also had to offset the two external hurdles: the high Canadian dollar and NAFTA. At the time, compared to the U.S. dollar, the Canadian dollar equaled 89 cents. That made purchasing American goods a lot cheaper. During most of the previous decade, the Canadian dollar had ranged only from 65 to 72 cents, which made it an anomaly then. When it went to 89 cents, the Americans discovered the Canadian market.

Additionally, NAFTA had reduced the 15 percent tariff on furniture to zero. This immediately removed the false barriers that had kept American companies away—the 15 percent tariff and the low Canadian dollar. That meant that the Americans could increase prices to the Canadians and still sell lower than Canadians could.

That also played the other way against Sklar Pepplar. We could no longer sell to the American market because of the value of the dollar. In fact, the loss of that market was what had finally plunged Sklar Pepplar into CCAA.

Now that we had the information we needed, our next task was to figure out how to solve those problems. With most of the customers, we had gone from number one to not even being seen on the horizon. Although Eaton's had been ready to share the problem, they were not as eager to buy our solution until we proved that it could work. We needed them more than they needed us. We would have to earn our way back.

VALUE PLUS

To get us moving, we decided to concentrate on one former Canadian customer, called the VIP Buying Group. Buying groups were made up of smaller stores that had banded together as a cooperative so they could buy in quantity. By 1992, they represented 147 retail stores (although several people owned more than one store).

"Why don't we get business from you?" we asked their representatives. "At one time, you had been our biggest customer."

"We don't need you anymore," one of them said candidly and recited essentially what we already had found out about American products.

"If we can provide the same quality, competitive prices, and a good delivery system, would you reconsider ordering from us?" we asked. "Sklar Pepplar is not only a Canadian company, but we've had a long history together."

Gord McDonald, their executive director, and Steve Brannif, the vice president of merchandising, worked with us in developing a product line for VIP. For us, it was a great moment and a big risk. They had nothing to lose. If they didn't like our products and services, they only had to say no.

"Yes," was all we needed to start moving. They didn't give us an order—and we hadn't asked for one—but they did agree to give us a chance. Now it was up to us to prove ourselves.

Immediately, we faced a threefold challenge. First, we had to lower the cost. We realized that meant cutting our costs in the manufacturing process so we could cut the retail price. We created a task force called Value Plus, which included members from every department involved, from engineering to purchasing to shipping.

This team became a highly energized and focused group of champions, all focused on the same prize. The stakes were high, and it was my job to tear down the barriers that got in their way. That team made a covenant with each other that they would do what was in the best interests of the team's goal, regardless of the impact on their individual jobs or departments.

They worked with suppliers to find ways to reduce the cost of fabric and yet maintain the high quality. They reduced the engineering lead-time from months to weeks, and they established a new way of building frames that drastically reduced cost. From shipping to purchasing, they reduced overall costs by more than $200, which translated into a $400 price reduction at retail.

Second, we wanted to increase the quality and design appeal of our products—while cutting costs. We didn't want just to *equal* the American products, but Sklar Pepplar was determined to match or surpass their fashion design, and their price, and maintain a quality advantage.

Third, we had to find the solution to rapid transportation. If the Americans could get an order and ship it to the retailer within four weeks, which was their usual delivery policy, we decided that we would have to do it in two.

Those were our challenges. If we succeeded in this single venture with the VIP Buying Group, we could position ourselves to retake the lead in the furniture business. We didn't delude ourselves. We had to make a lot of serious changes to become the values-oriented company we wanted. This pushed us to work closely with the three unions. They were—and rightly so—distrustful of us at first, because there had been a lot of friction in the past. So we invited the leadership from each union to learn about our goals. Once they understood fully what we were trying to do, they joined the team and allowed us to change many of the old work rules that led to inefficiency and waste.

Once we had the support of the union, our vice president of marketing, Jerry Modjeski, led the Value Plus team. I felt strongly that it would work because all of us were committed to the same goals. The Value Plus team flew to Saskatoon to meet with the VIP team. At first, we listened and asked questions until we figured out what they wanted. Then we discussed how we could provide those products.

Back in Toronto, I challenged the Value Plus team by laying out exactly what the VIP customers needed. "We're empowering you—the Value Plus team—to do this job. You'll get whatever resources you need to make it happen."

The team took me at my word and worked all spring on a line designed exclusively for the VIP Buying Group. When they showed the rest of us what they had come up with, every one of us liked the new line and supported it. They had designed four different sofa frames and three groups of living room wood furniture with entertainment centers. After the team completed the designs, the engineering group's job was to figure out ways to produce them faster and cheaper.

Because of the changes in material, we had to work with new suppliers. We chose those new suppliers carefully and according to the new values we were putting into place (as I'll explain more fully in the next chapter).

In the process, we developed a laser-cutting technology that would dramatically speed up production and greatly improve the productivity of the cutting room operation. We also designed a method to get the materials early enough at our plants so we could finish our work and get the furniture shipped out.

Finally, we worked with the shippers across Canada. At that time, it often took two weeks just to get our products from Toronto to Vancouver. Once we understood the problem, we created three distribution nodes across the country at Ontario, Saskatoon, and Vancouver. By pooling shipments into these nodes, we could maximize the use of bulk transport every week. The individual stores were serviced from those nodes, not from our plants in Ontario.

My team had done a good job of putting this all together, and I felt pumped up. Not only did we match everything American companies offered, but we actually increased the quality of the products over what our competitors offered.

We often referred to this as the "no guts, no glory" time, because the stakes were extremely high—the future at Sklar Pepplar depended on this one product line. In the furniture business, rumors continued to fly that Sklar Pepplar was going out of business, and some even thought that the doors had been padlocked. The media had made a big story of it when we had been forced into bankruptcy. Now that we were turning things around, though, they paid no attention. Sklar Pepplar had gone from headlines to an item on page three in the business section that said, "Sklar Pepplar is out of CCAA." It seemed as if the media delighted in the fact that the free trade was killing us. Because we were a well-known manufacturer, when we had closed plants in the 1980s, every closing became front-page news in Canada and even got sound bites on CBC television. Originally, Sklar Pepplar had six plants. By 1992, there were two.

As far as the public was concerned, the image of Sklar Pepplar of the past 50 years had vanished. Who wanted to buy furniture from a bankrupt or an almost-out-of-business company? We were determined to give them the answer.

Next came the advertising campaign. We did a co-op program with VIP to advertise the new product line on the front cover of their fall 1992 flyer, which was actually a small mail order catalogue. They produced 23 million such flyers and in a country of 28 million people, that's market dominance.

We agreed to the co-op because Sklar Pepplar needed the promotion. It was exciting that our Value Plus products would be on the front cover. We did the design and layout right, using a Canadian motif and even the national flag. We were trying to make a subtle statement that we could compete with—and even beat—the American furniture makers.

I'm an American, of course, and there I was in Canada building up the company. We had a marvelous sense of camaraderie that we brought to this thing. We wanted Sklar Pepplar employees to feel secure about their jobs. Also, we didn't want to beat the American companies by their failing, but rather by our succeeding.

From the old days when Lou Sklar had run the company, this would be the first time the leadership team did something together. There was a sense of accomplishment, and Value Plus came to mean something much more significant than the product line. It became the mantra for how we were to treat our customers, our suppliers, and each other.

We were now ready to show our new line to the VIP buyers. With it we would present our advertising plan through the flyer. Of course, we shot the cover photograph in the best possible light. On the inside, we also had three pages for our products. That's a lot of product visibility—and the VIP Buying Group absorbed most of the cost. We paid for the photography, but they paid for everything else.

The initial order would be worth $2.5 to $4 million for us. The reorder had a potential of $4 to $6 million. That meant a company that had been on the verge of bankruptcy only months before could jump from zero in sales to $6 million with one significant customer. The promotional aspects of the agreement were just as huge because all of our other customers would want to get on the bandwagon. Everybody loves to buy from the winners, and this program would clearly tell Canada that Sklar Pepplar was back.

The banks were beginning to consider us heroes because we had laid out plans and proved to them that we could compete with the bigger, more successful companies. They had a lot of money at stake in this.

The team needed to see the success. We'd broken down the old barriers within the organization and formed an ethical base by working in a covenant relationship. We were already tasting success.

STORM CLOUDS

The VIP Buying Group was to hold its 1992 meeting at the Camelback Lodge in Phoenix. During the three-day event, they would let us unveil our new line. It was a heady time for us.

Two days before the Phoenix meeting, I was in Toronto for our team to put together the final details of our presentation. Excitement filled the air. We had prototypes of everything we had advertised in the flyers.

Steve Brannif and Gord McDonald, the buying group executives, worked alongside us. This was an important time for them too, because they had put themselves on the line for us by presenting our prototypes to their board with enthusiastic endorsement. Everyone on their board liked our products.

We would have to ship samples to Phoenix and give them a mini-show at the annual meeting. Once buyers saw the line, they would then give us orders, which we would fill and ship in the fall.

Our dream was coming true.

At this point in Sklar Pepplar's new line, everything depended on timing. The flyer would hit homes in mid-September—timed that way because of Canadian Thanksgiving Day and then preparation for the Christmas season. That meant we had a small window of time for them to get out their flyers— between September 5 and 20. Next we faced tight schedules to get the furniture produced and shipped to them. When customers came into the store, they had to have the products right there on the floor. If we didn't actually have the new line to the stores, they wouldn't order for us to ship later.

The schedule was tight. We felt, however, that we could get the delivery on the store floors by September 1. We had everything in place to distribute across Canada.

Then came a problem.

It was one of those things none of us could have foreseen.

It tested our values and our commitment to our customers.

Two days before I left for Phoenix, Mike, our vice president of manufacturing, came into my office. "We can't do it," he said.

"What do you mean we can't do it?" I asked, shocked by his words.

"We can do everything, but we can't get it done in time for this flyer."

All of us were crestfallen as he explained that we had encountered unexpected problems with the new equipment. The delivery would take longer than we had planned for.

"It's probably not going to happen until mid-October or maybe even early November," he said. I sensed how difficult it was for him to speak, but he looked into my eyes and continued, "You told us to be covenantal, so I'm telling you now. We can and we will make the product, but we can't do it in the allotted time frame."

For almost half a day we tried to figure out what to do.

"You have to go there and sell it as though we can do it, and then we've just got to find a way to make it happen," was the expressed attitude of one team member.

"No, we can't do that," Mike replied. "Sklar Pepplar went that route, and look where we ended up. If we go to Phoenix, promise to deliver, and then we can't hold up our end of the agreement, we'll have egg on our face. Even worse, everyone will say, 'No wonder they nearly went bankrupt.'"

This news meant that the 147 VIP stores could buy the products offered in the catalogue, but they couldn't have them delivered by the date we had promised.

We *can* make it happen, part of me said as I listened to both sides. We can put on pressure and add employees.

Yes, but is it the right thing to do? argued another part of me.

This is a one-time thing, not a policy-setting decision, I argued silently.

Once I make a decision, then it becomes policy.

The internal arguments continued as the members of the Value Plus team spoke back and forth. We wanted to succeed and pull off a victory for Sklar Pepplar. How could we do it?

I stared at Mike as he made one more impassioned plea not to make promises we couldn't live up to. Mike had never advised me wrongly before, which is unusual for the furniture business. A lot of people in manufacturing put the best spin on everything to make it sound better and more optimistic. Although certainly not a pessimist, if Mike said it couldn't be done, then it couldn't.

"Do it! Make it happen!" insisted one of the marketing people. "We can force everyone to work harder until we get over this hump."

"No amount of forcing will get it done," Mike said. "We need at least six months lead. There just isn't enough time."

As the leader, the decision was mine. I had no idea what to do. I felt myself torn both ways, and still I couldn't make up my mind. There seemed no way to come out ahead on this one. If we missed getting the goods to them in time, we'd ruin the reputation we wanted to restore. If I told the truth, they might respect us for our integrity, but it wouldn't do us much good financially. In fact, it would probably be the last chance we would get to partner with a large customer on a project of this magnitude, and we desperately needed a win.

To make the situation worse, for the week after the Phoenix show, we had scheduled a meeting with the bank. I had expected to show them a $4 million order from VIP. I knew that would blow them away, and then they'd release additional money for plant acquisitions and growth. I needed the bank to think of Sklar Pepplar in terms of growth and not merely struggling for survival.

Another factor was the company's internal one. The Value Plus project had become a crucial matter, and we had been on the verge of a high level of success in morale and cooperation. Now what should we do?

A QUESTION OF CHARACTER

Before we left Toronto, I talked with the two men from VIP. "Here's the deal," I said. "We have this wonderful product and we have pictures of it. We have the fabrics and everything— except we can't ship the products on time. What should I do?"

My news shocked them. They got mad at Sklar Pepplar—and that was justified. We had promised and constantly reassured them that we could have everything done on time.

"You can't tell the group, Alan," one of the VIP officials said after he had calmed down. "If you do, VIP will never do business with Sklar Pepplar again."

"I don't know what you're going to do," the other added, "but you've got a problem, and you need to get it worked out." He really meant the same thing—fix it.

I didn't give them a decision about what I'd do because at that time I still didn't know.

Before the business meeting, those of us from Sklar Pepplar were supposed to mingle with and meet the VIP people, act friendly, and let them know we would be unveiling our top-quality products. I felt miserable, although I kept smiling and greeting everyone. Yet all the time I was thinking about how terrible the situation was. I couldn't blurt out the truth of what was going on.

At best, it gave me a few more hours to make a decision. That didn't help much. The next day I had to make my presentation of the new Sklar Pepplar line. I couldn't get any peace about what to say.

After a sleepless night, I went down to the business meeting. During the preliminaries, I sat on the platform and stared at the buyers, and I kept thinking. Representatives from 147 stores. What do I tell them?

Then, just minutes before they introduced me, a thought ran through my mind—a paraphrase of a verse from the Old Testament: "Don't be a man of unclean lips."

I knew exactly what those words meant. That morning, I had come face to face with one of the most important covenantal principles. If I lied or misled, I would be a man of unclean lips—a man without integrity, and the head of a company without integrity. I knew what I *had* to say.

After my introduction I began, "You would love for me to come up and tell you. . . ." I then shared with them all the things we had worked out. I produced pictures and gave figures, and provided details of the new line, the new manufacturing processes, and the new distribution partnership.

The excitement on their faces showed me they were sold on the program.

"You have to send your flyers out by September 20 and the photography has to go in next week. I know all the time lines on this." I took a deep breath and continued, "But I have to tell you we can't meet the deadline no matter how hard we try. I know that Steve and Gord are upset, because they worked hard to get this done." I couldn't look into the face of anyone there, but now that I had started, I knew I was doing the right thing. "Just two days before we came here, I learned that we can't have our new product line in your stores by September 1. We will bring out the product, and we will sell it, because the future of our company is riding on this new line. But we can't deliver to you by your deadline. Eaton's will buy and so will others, but we can't keep our commitment to you.

"I want to thank VIP, first of all, because you have forced us to be able to reinvent this company. I also want to ask your forgiveness, because all of us truly believed we were going to be able to do it. Not only must this be a big disappointment to you, but our people are extremely disappointed as well."

As I gazed across the audience, I could see their shock and then their disappointment. People grumbled and mumbled to each other, moved around in their chairs, and many angry faces glared at me. Sklar Pepplar had disappointed them many times in the past, which was why they originally had stopped doing business with us. Now I was doing it to them again.

"Again, I apologize," I said and stepped down. Nobody applauded as I turned away. Somehow I walked off that stage, but I felt as if I were an inch tall. Nobody came up to me, shook my hand, or patted me on the back. I saw anger on many faces as I walked through the convention hall.

I returned to my room where my wife, Sara, waited for me to report. I told her all that had happened.

"You did the right thing," she said and hugged me.

I knew that I had, but that didn't make me feel any better. It was also one of the most difficult things I ever had to do in my life.

I lay on the bed and closed my eyes. I didn't want to talk to anyone. As I replayed everything in my mind, I began to second-guess myself. Had I really done the right thing? Should I have pushed and demanded everyone at Sklar Pepplar to work over-time to pull it off? Should I have bluffed my way through? Despite the voices of doubt, I had an inner sense that what I did was what a covenant is all about. Always do what is in the best interest of the other, even if it might cost you heavily. I was at peace.

Because of flight schedules to Toronto, we couldn't leave immediately and had to wait until the next morning. I didn't sleep well for a second night. It wasn't because I questioned what I had done, it was because I still had to tell the Sklar Pepplar board and a room full of bankers the decision I had made.

After we packed our bags the next morning, I went downstairs to check out. To get to the front desk, I had to pass a garden area. By the time I got within view of that section, I realized I would have to walk past the executive committee of the VIP Buying Group. They were seated in plain sight, engaged in a deep discussion. I groaned inwardly; I didn't want to talk to anyone. What could I say anyway?

I didn't look at them and kept walking. They couldn't have missed seeing me as I crossed the wide atrium area within ten feet of them.

"Alan! Come over here." Gord raised his hand and beckoned. "We need to talk to you."

I forced a smile on my face and walked toward them. I almost laughed as I thought, well, they can't make me feel any worse than I already do.

A Scotsman named Ian was a member of the executive committee. Only later did I learn that he was not only a member and owned six stores, but he was one of the founders of the buying group. That made him a highly influential man with VIP.

Ian reached out and clasped my hand. With his Scottish brogue, he said, "You know, lad, you did exactly what Lou Sklar would have done in the old days. The reason we stopped doing business with Sklar Pepplar is because they lost that great sense of doing the right thing. But don't you be worrying. We're going to do a lot of business with Sklar Pepplar. You're a company of integrity again." He shook my hand and smiled.

"Thank you," I said and walked away.

As I approached the front desk, my spirits had lifted. I had done the right thing and at least Ian was commending me for it.

Once back in Toronto, although I didn't go back to the bank with millions of dollars worth of business, I did go back assured that I had done the right thing. The VIP Buying Group seemed to respect us, because they gave us a four-month extension— which was all we needed to turn things around.

One week later we took our Value Plus products program to Eaton's and they placed a large order. From there, we went to another chain called Leon's, and made another big sale. We next took a really big chance by crossing the border into the United States, and they also bought our products. Everywhere we offered our Value Plus line, sales boomed.

As Ian had predicted, my confession in Phoenix didn't end Sklar Pepplar's relationship with VIP. In fact VIP's second catalogue of the year—the spring tabloid as they called it—featured our Value Plus program. The sales were phenomenal and surpassed what we had expected six months earlier. Even more important, we had acted honorably. Their response showed they respected us for that. Without ever mentioning our commitment to covenant with them, they had experienced the power and impact of that covenant firsthand.

Since then, the VIP Buying Group bought two other furniture chains and has become Canada's largest buying group. Oh, and yes, as of this writing they continue to be Sklar Pepplar's largest single customer.

We had accomplished what we set out to do. We were a company of integrity. Looking back, it would have been easier to compromise, mislead, or lie—all commonly accepted practices in the world of business. By maintaining our commitment to ourselves and to our customers, we had moved into the level of being beyond world class.

CHAPTER FOUR

BUILDING COVENANTAL RELATIONSHIPS

When we serve our customers with excellence—that is, covenantly—we're applying beyond-world-class principles. If we do it right, such an attitude spreads throughout the company and it affects everybody. This means that serving with excellence isn't a separate activity or something we remind ourselves to do. It's not part of a values-training program. When we understand the importance of every person within the organization being part of the covenantal agreement, we are already moving into this concept.

Instead of spending vast amounts of effort to figure how to make this work, it's easier if we accept the fact that it's a matter of applied learning. Once people grasp what's expected of them and see it modeled around them, they begin to apply the principles. (This is discussed more fully in Chapter 8.)

In other words, when everybody is committed to covenantal concepts, such attitudes become the culture of the organization. This may sound impossible when I use words such as "everyone," but once the culture is set, the attitude spreads quickly. I've seen it demonstrated in too many corporations not to believe in this method.

Beyond-world-class principles not only transform the character of the company, but people within the company change—which shows that this isn't just superficial behavior or a form of imposed conduct. These changes show themselves in the way employees approach customers or suppliers. When the people within the organization embrace these powerful principles, everything within the work and life of the company is done as part of an integrated whole and nothing is a separate component.

The simplest way to grasp this idea is to observe how it works in practical ways. If we treat our coworkers with respect, it's not a stretch to see that we'll also treat our customers and suppliers with that same level of respect.

Let's look at the inverse of this concept. Do we think that employees who treat coworkers rudely will have instant transformations to enable them to act respectfully toward customers and suppliers? Probably not. People are remarkably consistent in the way they treat others. It's also true that when those within an organization treat others with dignity, the recipients respond in the same way. They prove the wisdom of the old saying, "What goes around, comes around."

This is an ongoing process, and if we're committed to building covenantal relationships, we set the example; others learn from us and apply the principles in reacting to each other. Our growing and changing demonstrates itself by the way we treat suppliers and customers. It's just that simple.

Before we go any further, I want to make it clear that I'm not simply advocating a few cosmetic changes, or teaching a few how-to-win techniques, or showing ways to manipulate those we want to influence. The goal of beyond-world-class concepts is to live by these values.

There is an axiom in psychology that says everything we do expresses who we are and the values we hold. The clothes we wear, the cars we drive, and the words we choose all reflect our individual attitudes. If we embrace beyond-world-class principles, they manifest themselves quite naturally in the way we treat others.

In business today, perhaps that sounds naïve and simplistic. *But the principles work.*

I'm going to cite examples of companies where they're committed to building those value-based relationships. If it works with these companies, why won't it work anywhere?

Answer: It will.

This doesn't mean it's easy or simple. Even once we grasp the concept and begin to implement covenant relationships, it requires determination, vigilance, and a concerted effort to promote the concepts within every area. It becomes an experience of ongoing and consistent learning.

Accepting beyond-world-class principles also grants freedom to everyone. We don't have to live by two standards or two sets of principles. We have only one set of principles and they apply to everyone. We live by these principles when we deal with customers, but they're just as important when we work with the person at the next desk. They apply to those we buy from as well as our supervisors, managers, and executives. I'm an employee, and whether I lead, manage, or follow, in a beyond-world-class company, I am responsible to live covenantly—regardless of where I stand on the corporate ladder.

It is unfortunate, but we haven't taught such principles to some of the top leaders in the business world. They keep trying to heal only the symptoms of the sickness without getting to the cause.

What typically happens in companies is that the leadership says, "Hmm, morale is low, so we need to pump it up." Instead of seeing low morale as symptomatic of more serious underlying problems, they see it as the cause of the situation.

How do they fix the problem? They bring in motivational speakers and business gurus. While those outside speakers may score a few points in one area, and perhaps some of the information may even carry over into another area, what they rarely provide is a tied-down, values-oriented teaching that holds each person responsible for his or her actions.

To state it another way, despite all the workshops, seminars, and learning opportunities, most of the training isn't integrated. Yet, when organizations begin to integrate the simple principles of covenant relationships, everything changes. Relationships improve on every level—with customers, suppliers, leaders, and coworkers. Employees begin to enjoy coming to work. This excitement is generated at all levels within the company and even the person who answers the telephone sets an enthusiastic tone for customers.

ONE-WAY COVENANTS

Here's an example of how one-way covenants can negatively impact your company. A large organization, whom I can't identify for obvious reasons, was in deep trouble. They called our company—Corporate Development Institute (CDI). We investigated and discovered that their problems actually were worse than they were willing to admit.

The CEO had heard about the concept of covenant relationship and knew enough about it to say, "This is a great idea and we want to use it here."

It took us three weeks of working with the organization before we found out how badly their business had floundered. (They have since filed for Chapter 11, but in their reorganization, they already are implementing beyond-world-class principles.)

Their biggest problem was simple. About 70 percent of their business came from one customer, a computer giant. That's not the healthiest relationship (to throw so much effort into one place), and to make it worse, that corporation wasn't covenantal.

In this case, I'm not identifying the people to protect the guilty. I'll refer to the company that called us as Acme. The situation worked like this: Because of the large amount of business Acme received from the computer corporation, they built a new plant in Texas and added a substantial number of people to their workforce.

This expansion put Acme into debt. They continued to pay their bills as they came due, but their expansion program depended solely on the business from that single megacorporation. In preparing themselves for the increase in business from the giant corporation, Acme had spent nearly $20 million on the plant, equipment, and salaries of an additional 1,100 employees to become fully operational.

Then the problems struck. They began when the computer giant decreased the amount of business they gave Acme. The downturn became so severe that Acme had already laid off 300 employees before they contacted us.

Acme tried to function within the concept of fulfilling their vision of what a covenant company should be. They didn't have it quite right, but they were trying. For years, they had said, "We don't lay off employees. We treat our people as valued employees and we're a long-term provider."

That commitment came about because when they had been a fairly new company in the 1960s, they had been forced to lay off a large number of employees. It had been a heart-wrenching experience for the owner and the board. The leaders determined they would never let that happen again. They were fully committed to keeping their employees and to be viewed as a company that didn't lay off workers.

As I've said, their expansion in Texas forced them to borrow. The customer paid on time—that wasn't the issue. In fact, for a short time, the computer firm increased the amount of business. The problem was that the customer had given Acme a verbal agreement for their next three years' business, but they had never provided a written contract.

Based on verbal agreements alone, Acme had gone into debt. Although they repeatedly asked for a written contract, the computer giant procrastinated, assuring Acme, "Oh, yes, we'll give you a contract soon."

The contract never materialized, but Acme went forward in good faith anyway.

One day, an executive in the computer company asked, "Why are we doing this huge volume of business with Acme? Can't we do it cheaper elsewhere?" The corporation did a cost analysis and—here is where they showed they were not a covenantal organization—they decided to study what Acme did, learn everything they could from them, and then set up their own division, thus cutting out Acme.

For nearly a year, they allowed Acme to continue, but they carefully monitored their activities and learned all the details. Once Acme had completed its expansion and the plant was fully operational with all the bugs worked out, the computer people went to a competitor of Acme and asked, "Could you do this project in Mexico?" They didn't inform Acme that they were allowing them to be the prototype and that they planned to renege on their verbal agreement and dump them.

Once the other company agreed to the arrangement, using the much cheaper Mexican labor, the computer people went to Acme and said, "We're going to turn our business over to a plant in Mexico. You have 60 days to meet the price they have given us."

Of course, Acme couldn't match the price because the figures were so low that Acme would have lost money if they had agreed.

"Too bad," the computer giant said. In 60 days, they took all of their business away from Acme. But worse than diverting their work, they had used Acme as the model, allowed them to develop the system, and then provided that valuable information to Acme's competitor. As a result, Acme had to close the Texas plant and lay off the final 800 people.

Too late, Acme learned that although they were a covenantal company, it wasn't enough. Because they had worked with people who were not covenantal, they had violated their own commitment not to lay off employees.

They also realized—again too late—that the customer covenant is an important aspect of operating by beyond-world-class principles. As they restructure, they are stressing (and remembering) the importance of making sure their customers also are willing to work on covenantal principles. The power in a covenant is that it is mutually binding and mutually beneficial.

This isn't to speak against doing business without contracts or guarantees. But it's a warning about being careful and especially in being covenantal with those we work with, buy from, or sell to.

Had Acme studied the history of that giant corporation, they would have known that long ago the organization had developed a pattern of abusing its suppliers. A number of giant corporations do that and get away with it. Even though we see it all the time and even warn ourselves, the lure of the "home run" order often blinds us to the potential downside of doing business in covenant with someone who only operates by the covenant of convenience. Covenantal companies need to avoid doing business with such organizations.

VISION AND COVENANT ALIGNMENT

The Acme situation was a negative example; here's an example with a more positive outcome.

When S.D. Myers Company acquired SunOhio Company, their CEO, Dana Myers, wanted us to help them to function as a beyond-world-class company. Both companies were in the same business, with many similarities, yet each had competencies in different areas. It was a great fit for the two to become one. At CDI, we worked with their two key executives, Dana Myers and Dale Bissonnette, to smooth out the details of the merger.

Among other things, I interviewed leaders and talked quite a bit with the chief operations officer as well as vice presidents and managers of both sales and marketing divisions. I kept pounding home to them this fact: "You need to do what's in the best interest of the customer. But you do that *by fulfilling your vision of the company.*"

This second part seemed to come as a surprise. Finally, one executive said, "So that means we can be somewhat selfish in this. It's not just bending over backward for customers, is it?"

"Exactly right," I replied. "You have to fulfill your vision. That comes first. You do what's in the best interest of customers *as long as it aligns with that vision.* If they're asking you to violate your vision, that's not a covenantal relationship."

I pointed out that this principle places a responsibility on every employee—from the CEO down to the people on the loading dock. Each one must be able to live a life that fulfills that vision on behalf of the company and the customer.

I wanted them to be able to get a true and affirmative answer if they asked any employee, "Do you have good relationships with others in the company? Do you treat others in the company the way you want to be treated? Does your supervisor treat you that way?"

This is an overlooked principle, and many otherwise good companies don't see its importance. We need to promote this concept of involving everyone to become part of a beyond-world-class company. One way is to start teaching this concept at employee entry-levels. In fact, we now refer to this as part of our Employee Foundations.

The results? When the principles become second nature to every member within the organization, companies are revolutionized. "No one ever laid this out to me before," one supervisor said. "It just makes good sense."

It does make good sense. In the early days, I started teaching the concepts by stressing that it was the responsibility of leaders to serve their employees. That wasn't wrong, but it wasn't enough. Some of them assumed I meant acting kind, being friendly, always smiling, and trying a few other manipulative gimmicks. Consequently, although some leaders caught the message, many didn't.

In recent years, I've learned to say these things stronger, clearer, and more comprehensively. For instance, I now stress responsibility for each person. Every employee needs to tie in with the covenant.

As I've continued to work with various organizations, I've realized that the responsibility is everyone's task—every employee needs to be covenantal with their coworkers, with customers, and with suppliers. They have to be willing to serve and to be served. They must learn to embrace this matter of mutuality. This principle of mutuality becomes part of the guiding principle that allows us to fulfill our covenant with our customers.

Under the old system of helping companies, we had someone teach employees a value model and talk a little about the importance of character, and then we explained the company's predetermined core values. For instance, we'd point out that one value is integrity and we'd carefully explain what we meant by that term.

The next day, the employees would return to their jobs. They had learned a lot of definitions, but they still didn't know how to apply those values.

We congratulated ourselves, believing we had helped them. Too often, we made up pithy little statements and hung them in the break room. We ordered plaques with motivational sayings and put them where everyone would have to see them. Sometimes we used cartoons like *Herman* or *Dilbert* to point out those values. In all of this, we hoped that because they had training they'd read those words when they sat down for coffee. We were sure they'd ponder those clever cartoons and put the principles into practice. Most of the time, if the sayings were funny, they'd read them. If they were serious, everyone ignored them.

If we went to what I call the successory store, we bought wonderful large pictures of Snoopy the beagle with a wise saying. Another would have a different character, but they were all supposed to teach and impress principles. Supposedly, employees read all those things, paused, reflected, and then exclaimed, "Wow! Now I understand."

Even if those methods had worked (and they did not), they still didn't teach employees how to apply the core values we wanted them to live by. We kept laying more information on them and urging them to adhere to the values.

The reality is that the leaders didn't adhere to the values we taught. If they didn't absorb what we were teaching, they couldn't model the sought-after behavior. And the employees continued to follow the old examples their leaders set.

As I struggled with this, it led me to what I call the base line. Negatively, it goes like this: If just one person fails to perform according to the core values of the company and continues to work there, something happens to the entire organization. In subtle ways, one person lowers the standard.

For instance, we say as a matter of being covenantal: "We will be honest with our customers. We will not lie." But if one employee lies and gets away with it, then being truthful is no longer a company value. Soon others learn that they too can lie and it doesn't hurt the company very much. If lying even seems to help the company get more business or increase its profits, it lowers the standard even more.

I can envision a manager lying to a customer as he stands next to the wall where a large poster proclaims, "Integrity is our highest value." The manager justifies his actions by thinking, it's just this one time.

This lying-if-it-helps-the-company mentality leads to what we call *situational values*—the normal climate in corporate America. Situational values say that everything is relative, and there are no absolute values in business. We base our actions and attitudes on what is currently happening. We make decisions on what will grant our company the most immediate profit. Even worse, in companies with the unspoken situational values, there is no ultimate standard for anything. How can employees know which values to apply? How can they know what conduct is expected of them?

All this is to say that giving more information and just explaining principles hasn't worked very well, and it certainly hasn't produced the desired results. That's rather sad when we consider that corporations annually spend millions of dollars in training and motivating their employees, buying plaques, and printing signs.

If that approach doesn't work, what does?

THE CUSTOMER-COVENANT MODEL

From our experience, we know one thing that does work well. We call it the *customer covenant model*. We've proven its effectiveness with many companies, large and small. We start by changing our approach and putting our covenant with customers right up in front: "This is where we draw the line. These are the terms that we will abide by."

Before I go further, it's important to point out that there isn't just one single customer. We usually mean groups—individuals and companies. If we treat them as one group, we'll have difficulty working with these principles. In fact, when we lump them into a single, all-look-alike group, we add problems for ourselves.

For instance, if we're a McDonald's, it's difficult to draw a mental picture of one customer, so we do customer groups. The suburban, metro-Atlanta breakfast group differs from the breakfast group in downtown Peoria. If we can picture that person or group, we then can focus on their needs. As we do, we create *policies* for each customer or group of customers.

Here's what I want to make clear in identifying our customers: *We set policies for different customer groups; our principles remain the same for everyone.*

When we focus on our individual customers, we can see that their needs are different. For example, we set specific policies for industrial customers, and we have another set of policies for utility customers. Customers in Charleston have different requirements than those in Boise. We set policies according to customer needs and even those needs change. When I explain this concept to employees, they have no trouble grasping the idea.

To take it further, not only do we have different policies, but we also may have different products and services for various customer groups. It's like cooking bacon, eggs, and grits for breakfast for someone in Chattanooga, but a Miami customer might want a burrito. Both are breakfast customers and it's the same company—but our customers place different orders according to their wants.

What is common to both customers? They want fast, friendly service, even though one may ask for the order in English and the other in Spanish. One of the most persistent problems many large companies face, including McDonald's, is lack of consistency in service and in principles.

As we set policies for the various customers, the products also change, and that means our policies will probably change too, but the values never do. We apply the same principles to every customer whether in Boise, Peoria, Birmingham, Chattanooga, Atlanta, or Miami. When this happens, our principles become inviolate standards.

"Yes, that makes sense," a middle manager in Ohio once said to me. "It doesn't matter where they live or what they buy, we cater to their needs with different products, but we stay within our principles in setting the policies."

He said it well.

To many, this concept seems obvious, but everyone doesn't see it at first. In fact, many have resisted because of their own inflexibility. That is, they insist that the only way to do business is to treat everyone exactly the same way. They call that being fair. I challenge their thinking.

"If we change policies, we don't have integrity," one salesman said to me.

"No, just the opposite," I said. "We don't have integrity unless we can change policies. Integrity means we refuse to shift our principles."

Here's the example I gave him. Suppose I work with one large company and realize they can pay for their goods in 30 days, so I tell them that's acceptable. I also do business with another customer that has a slower turnaround on products. We work with that customer and finally say, "Okay, you can take 90 days to pay, but this added cost of business will be reflected in the price you pay." Each agrees to pay within their own period of time.

I have just set two different policies, and I have still maintained integrity. The principle is that both will pay as they agreed. However, if I don't enforce my principles and make certain that both companies abide by our agreement, that's when I lack integrity.

The covenant model works when our employees understand the difference between products, policies, and principles.

BUSINESS-TO-BUSINESS AND BUSINESS-TO-CONSUMER MODELS

Let's take this further. There are two models to work with in this setting of principles: business to business (B2B) and business to consumer (B2C). McDonald's is a B2C company.

S.D. Myers, however, is a B2B company that sells to another company, which still isn't the final consumer. They sell electrical services to utility companies, and those utility companies then sell services to their customers, who are the consumers.

This is where different policies are most important. I've watched many B2B companies go out of business—probably more than B2C types—and it usually happens for one basic reason. Even though I know the answer, which we'll get to soon, I usually ask one question from the leaders of B2B companies that have crashed: "What happened?"

"Cash flow problems," is the typical answer.

That's not the answer, it's only the result—no cash, no business. Here's the real reason: They have not been covenantal with their customers. To be covenantal means that both buyers and sellers acknowledge and accept responsibility. To covenant with customers doesn't mean we'll behave stupidly and allow ourselves to be taken advantage of, or that we ignore the agreements we make.

This also means B2B companies must choose the right companies to work with. That is, they shouldn't agree to work with just any company. Whenever I've said this, I get resistance. Too many like to think that we're being irresponsible and fiscally foolish if we don't grab every customer who comes to us.

I think it's exactly the opposite: We need to be selective. One major reason companies have crashed is their lack of choosing the right people to covenant with. To become a covenantal organization we must say, "I will find people who understand what I'm doing. They know they can depend on me to fulfill my obligations, and I know I can depend on them to do what they promise."

That is, being covenantal means varying our products and services to meet customers' needs. It also means working only with those who will honor their end of the covenant—that is, they will pay as they have agreed.

We need to make certain that our policies are fair and flexible enough, but we also have to make it clear that we have inviolate principles and everyone in the company lives by them. Thus, we can say to our customers, "You tell us what you will do and we'll tell you how we'll serve you, and this will become a covenant."

Too few B2B startup companies insist on that open dialogue of making the terms clear. This is far more than making a profit or not going out of business. It is serving the customers' best interests—but that serving is done in alignment with the vision, purpose, and guiding principles of the company. *In alignment with* is the key phrase.

It isn't serving the best interests of our customers to allow them, for instance, not to pay on time. If we do, eventually we might go out of business. If we think only of their best interests, whether or not they're in alignment with our principles, then why not give everything to them? Wouldn't that be in their best interest? We'll give away all our products, our services—whatever they want—and charge them nothing. In fact, why don't we give them $100 per product? That's in their best interest, isn't it?

Okay, that's obviously stupid, but I've seen the principle violated too often because companies haven't realized that they've been giving away their products.

Doing what is in the best interest of the customer is correct—but it must always be done while fulfilling the mission and vision of our company. Before we start to buy from or sell to another company, we need to pull back and ask, "Does this supplier or customer help us fulfill the vision of our company?"

That's what every employee needs to consider. Everyone in the workforce needs to ask, "By working with them this way, will it help us fulfill our vision?"

If the employee can't answer yes, it's better not to do business with them. If they won't covenant with us, we don't want them as our customer. This isn't turning away business—it's turning away loss. If we go ahead, they'll eventually take advantage of us. And if we allow them to violate our covenant, we put our own company at risk.

EVERYONE'S BEST INTEREST

The definition of a covenantal strategy is doing what is in the best interest of everyone—customers, suppliers, bankers, and employees. That is, we want to do what is in the best interest of all involved simultaneously.

If, however, our purpose is merely to create profit, there's no significant covenantal value in that. But if our purpose is financial gain coupled with intrinsic values, then we have moved toward becoming a beyond-world-class company.

Earlier, I showed how this worked with the Canadian company, Sklar Pepplar. Their purpose was first to survive and then to succeed. That's a valued purpose. As part of that they would also keep families employed. If they paid their bills on time, they helped the economy. So that's a good purpose—success for an organization. But the profit factor wasn't enough.

Too many people think covenanting means that we become soft and easygoing, and that we constantly forgive or play the role of doormat. That's wrong. Covenant means we expect everyone to respect standards and values.

We expect our employees to do what is in the best interest of the company on behalf of a higher purpose. It's a matter of quid pro quo. In a beyond-world-class company, when we hire individuals, we explain the nature of covenant. This changes the way we recruit as well as the way we train.

If we work covenantly, we apply the same principles in our dealings with our customers. The next section provides an example of this.

"HOW COULD YOU LET THIS HAPPEN?"

Wayne and Lynnette Baum of Lansing, Michigan, own an excavating company. They came to me after they had heard me speak at a convention about being covenantal. At that time, their company was close to bankruptcy and so were they personally.

"You should be making money," I said when I first studied their business. "Something is wrong here."

After some discussion, Lynnette explained the most serious problem. "We have one particular customer who won't pay regularly and that has forced us to keep getting loans." She went on to say that the customer—one of their largest accounts— owed them for 22 months of outstanding receivables. "They average 262 days before they pay their bills."

Her revelation shocked me. "That means that all of the money this customer owes you is almost a year old before you collect. It should be 30 days net."

The Baums are a really fine, ethical couple who care about their employees and are kind people.

To continue operating their company, they had started to borrow money. Before long, they had mortgaged their company's assets as well as their house. It still wasn't enough, and they continued to borrow from the bank.

"I keep telling that company to pay," Wayne said. "I keep sending them overdue notices, but they still don't pay on time."

"Did you try to work with them on paying?" I asked.

"Well, not really. We've had no choice, because we don't want to cut them off," Wayne said. "They're just about our biggest customer."

I shook my head, "Maybe so, but they're forcing you into bankruptcy. You have to do something drastic just to be able to stay in business." After we talked a little more, I said flatly, "You need to apply covenant relations with that customer."

Wayne agreed, but wasn't sure how to go about it.

"You start by going to that customer and explaining the nature of covenant. If you commit to go and do excavating work for them and bill them for the rock you supply, you promise to do that work with excellence. You will do it within their time requirements, and you promise to do whatever you can to meet their needs. Your program will be good for them. However, their part of the covenant is that they will pay you within 30 days. Have you done that with them?"

"Well, they kind of know what we do and this is business. But no, we haven't done that."

At first, Wayne wanted to write a letter and explain all the ways they had failed to pay their bills and that, consequently, they were forcing him to go out of business.

I urged him not to send that letter but to insist on a face-to-face conversation with the president. "The problem isn't your customer's fault. You're the one that violated the covenant."

Wayne was silent and then added, "I don't understand why they treat us this way. I've supplied them. They're the ones who aren't paying."

"That's right, but your responsibility was to hold them to their obligation. Go and see your customer—face to face. Don't talk to the buyer or a second in command. Meet directly with the owner."

He agreed that he would do that.

"Then you say to him, 'I have to apologize. I didn't explain my expectations to you, and here's what I've allowed your company to do. I need to ask your forgiveness.'" Then I told him to explain the nature of the covenant.

Wayne did just as I suggested.

The first reaction from the owner was, "How did you let us get 262 days behind? We owe you hundreds of thousands of dollars. How could you let us do that?"

Without giving Wayne a chance to reply, the owner called in his chief financial officer as well as one of his project managers. "How did we get this way with these folks?"

The CFO answered, "Well, you know, we first pay those companies that put the most pressure on us. Right now our cash is tight, and we have some problems collecting from our customers, and . . . ."

"But 262 days? That's embarrassing." He turned to Wayne, "I appreciate your coming in. I like this idea of covenant, and it sounds like a good thing. I'd like to learn to do that with my customers."

After they discussed the immediate situation for several minutes, he said, "So what you're saying to me is that we need to pay you in 30 days, and if we agree, you'll feel okay, and you'll keep supplying us?"

Wayne agreed, of course.

"Right now that may be a little difficult for us. But if we could pay you in 45 days instead of 30, would that work? That would help us immensely."

"I could live with that," Wayne replied. At that point, any schedule of payment would have satisfied him.

"From now on," the president promised, "for everything we order from you, we will pay you within 45 days." Next they talked about the $400,000 debt. "We don't have the money to pay for that now, but we want to catch up as quickly as possible. Here's what we can do. If we agreed to pay you $10,000 a week until we catch up, would that be satisfactory? That will still take us 40 weeks to catch up, but it would show our good faith."

"That'll work," Wayne said.

"If we can do better than that," the owner offered, "we will. But I can promise that you'll get the $10,000 every week."

The president did even better than he had promised. In less than eight months they had paid Wayne the entire $400,000. In turn, Wayne was able to pay his vendors and creditors on a timely and covenantal basis.

This illustrates how covenants work. They do work when all parties clearly understand the principles. As in this case, it was when both parties agreed to the same terms. What Wayne had to learn—and this is true with many companies—is that even though they want to be covenantal, they violate the covenant themselves when they allow such things to happen.

The power of the covenant is that it links the customer, supplier, and all the employees. It becomes a chain of interdependency. Those in a beyond-world-class company know that all parties have to stay covenantal for these links to strengthen and benefit everyone.

CHAPTER FIVE

SEEING THE CUSTOMER'S FUTURE
Four Power Questions

How much do you think about your customers' future? If you're like most businesspeople, the answer is, "Probably not enough."

Yet this is a crucial concept in the strategy of a beyond-world-class company. Our customers buy from us and we're concerned about our profit and our future. But what about *their* profit and their future business? How about in the months ahead? What about five years from now? Or ten years? The more we can focus on their future, the more we can enhance our own company's future. This principle not only applies to our customers but also to our suppliers. Their future links directly with ours.

THE PROBLEM WITH ASSUMPTIONS

In opening up this issue of looking at the needs of our customers, here are three false assumptions we need to face:

1. We cannot assume that our customers know where they're going.

2. We cannot assume that our customers' industries are stable and consistent just because they've been stable and consistent in the past. (Every industry undergoes enormous change.)

3. We cannot assume that our customers don't want our help.

If we turn number three around and assume customers want our help, we can eliminate all three fallacies.

Although there are always exceptions, how can we know until we offer to help? As we ask our customers questions and show genuine concern for their future, we're also helping to enhance our own growth. We can help them move toward continuous solutions—to prepare for the long-term delays and detours as well as the directional changes that will occur before they get to the red light. If they succeed, they will have many green lights ahead of them.

If we're willing to ignore these false assumptions, what do we do next? We offer to help our customers. How do we help? Because most people function from the perspective of their own goals and ambitions, it's sometimes difficult for them to turn their attention from themselves to ponder the needs of their customers.

We've learned at Corporate Development Institute (CDI) that one simple device is to start with four power questions. "Go to your customers," we tell clients. "Ask these questions and it may amaze you when you see the results."

When we went to the customers on behalf of a company that wanted to be covenantal, without exception the first response was, "No one ever asked us that before."

THE FOUR POWER QUESTIONS

Here are the four power questions we devised to help customers directly. When asking these questions, the companies we worked for benefited indirectly by obtaining the good will of their customers:

1. What changes must you make to meet the needs of your customers in the future?

2. What are the most significant threats—long-term and short-term—to your industry?

3. What are the three most significant opportunities that you have to serve your customers in the future?

4. How will you meet all the challenges in your industry?

When we first started asking questions on behalf of our clients, we encountered suspicion—and why wouldn't there be skepticism about our motives? "What's the catch? What do you get out of this?" we often heard.

Initially, our clients' customers quite rightly questioned why we wanted to help them. However, as we worked with them, they realized we had decided to tie in our future growth with theirs. Once they saw that we had their good in mind *as well as our own,* they were pleased to have us.

I want to add here, that we never tried to appear altruistic. We wanted our business to grow and to profit, and we did it by linking our growth and profit with theirs. Our openness was a key factor in convincing them.

Let's examine the four questions in detail.

1. What Changes Must You Make to Meet the Needs of Your Customers in the Future?

"I have no idea," one business owner responded to our first question.

His answer wasn't unusual. Far too many companies focus so much on racing down the highway and passing all the other cars, they hardly seem aware that they will hit traffic jams, detours, and maybe even a few speed bumps around the next curve. This question pushes the business owner to look for those conditions that will slow them down or force them off the road.

"What changes are you going to have to make in your company to meet the needs of your customers?" We kept pushing that question, and while they reflected, we added, "If we can understand the changes you need to make, we can understand you're starting to think about *your* customers' needs. And if we understand your customers' needs, we can help you meet them."

I want to be clear about what I hope you'll accomplish if you try these power questions. They aren't just to make more money for your company or to get more of their business or get a lower rate from them. Instead, they are to make that customer a covenant partner. A customer for life. If you do that, everyone wins.

When business leaders finally answered the first question—and sometimes it took some probing—they'd say, "Well, here's what we have to do."

Their answers showed us the issues they were concerned about. By asking questions and listening to their answers, they shared with us the growing demands of their customers, and those that would force them to make changes to keep them. They gave us opportunities to partner with them in those changes. We also wanted to help them become more flexible and to react quicker to market changes. We then began to help them explore how to make those changes.

2. What Are the Most Significant Threats — Long Term and Short Term—to Your Industry?

Perhaps I can make this second question clearer with an illustration involving the owner of KDA Design, Joe Hall. Located in Atlanta, KDA was in the construction industry and designed, manufactured, and furnished bank branch offices.

When we met, their major customers were Nations Bank and Trust Company and Bank of America. KDA selected sites for future bank branches, bought the sites, and built the buildings. They were the best in the southeast at doing that. Around 1994 and 1995, however, the banking industry began to make significant changes with the growing importance of automated teller machines (ATMs) and the introduction of Internet banking.

When they contacted us, they told us, "We want to grow. Help us know how to do that."

When I went to see Joe, I asked him the previous four power questions.

He stared at me and shook his head. "I have no idea how to answer any of the questions."

We didn't know either, but we worked with Joe and created a survey. "What are your most significant long-term and short-term threats?" we asked.

Rather than just letting Joe and his top people tell me what they thought, we sent people out to banking customers. Who would know better than the people who used the branch banking offices? We asked bank managers and bank employees for their answers, so that Joe could see this from many different perspectives.

The most commonly mentioned threat banking customers saw was the Internet. "It is going to change the style of banking." They saw this in 1995 before many people had even purchased computers or gotten online.

"But how?"

"We're not sure we'll need branch banks anymore," the customers said.

After looking at the results of the surveys, we asked Joe, "Do you want to go where your customers are going? Do you want to grow and plan to build more buildings if they're going to have to close down branch buildings?"

That answer was obvious. So what did KDA need to do?

Joe's company had been going full force in erecting buildings, and they realized they needed to slow down and rethink
what they were doing.

"How can we continue to serve the banking industry when
they're probably going to have to shut down branches?" We
helped him to ask and answer this question.

Consolidation posed a big threat, and Joe knew that intuitively. When he asked bank managers and business owners,
they admitted they were terrified over the threat. Some feared
they'd end up tearing down the buildings, or at best, selling
them.

Joe realized that the market share of bank buildings—his
industry—was going to shrink. So how could he grow in a
shrinking industry? He didn't want to grow where future profitability would go down. That was his dilemma and Joe did his
research. I'll discuss those results after we review the final two
questions.

3. What Are the Three Most Significant Opportunities That You Have to Serve Your Customers in the Future?

Next we went to the banking people and asked, "What
opportunities do you have?"

Obviously, Internet posed the greatest threat, but they realized that it was also their best opportunity if they could figure
out how to take advantage of it.

"We have to learn how to do Internet banking," one bank
officer said. "We have to revamp how we approach branch
banking." He also realized that even if branches weren't going
away, they would change. (Although they recognized more than
three opportunities, I'm limiting this example to one of them.)
We next examined the final question.

4. How Will You Meet All the Challenges in Your Industry?

"So how will you meet these changes?" Joe asked bankers.

"We don't know," one of them confessed. Despite a bluster of words, most of them admitted they were as perplexed as he was.

After Joe (and our researchers) collected the information we needed, we sat down with him and his leadership team. I want to make this clear: I came on the scene only as a change agent. I was the only one present who knew practically nothing about banking; I knew even less about construction. That was also my advantage. I didn't have a lot of prejudicial thinking to push aside, and I wasn't locked into predetermined answers.

"Let's be sure about this," I said. "You want to grow with the banking industry?" I asked, because that was one of the things Joe and the others had said they wanted.

"Yes," they affirmed.

"Then you must restructure." As a change agent, it was my responsibility to help them see what this meant. "You're not going to grow in this business if you continue to make banking your total focus."

That may not have been the answer they wanted to hear, but they listened when I asked, "So what is it your company does—that is, what do you do that we can put into the equation toward continuous solutions development?" As they pondered this, I added, "Let's simplify this. Tell me, in the most basic language, what you do."

"We build boxes—brick boxes . . . " someone answered and laughed.

"Good. Now, who else needs boxes? That is, what other industry is actually growing and because of that growth needs *more* brick boxes?"

Silence filled the room for perhaps 30 seconds before someone asked, "How about the health care industry? They're building more managed-care homes, aren't they? And what about assisted living centers?"

"Good idea," I encouraged.

From then on, their enthusiasm picked up. Within an hour they had created a vision that used their competencies and expertise and began to understand how to take their already existing construction business and apply their expertise to the managed-care field.

Someone else mentioned what we called "doc-in-the-box" buildings—the small, independent businesses that had sprung up in metropolitan areas, such as emergency clinics where people could see a doctor within minutes.

As they continued discussing this possibility, they realized that they lacked one thing before they could move into doc-in-the-box construction and managed-care facilities—they didn't have the medical competency. They couldn't begin to build any such facilities until they knew the needs and demands of that industry.

They then took the next smart steps. They contracted with a company to do the interiors. After they consulted together to select the sites, Joe's company erected the buildings. Within a short time they were ready to build two new types of buildings—and it came about after they began to ask about their customers' future.

When they asked further questions about clinics and health care facilities, those in that business gave them an obvious response: "We have to be located in areas where people need us."

As they looked forward, they saw that they had to consider more than managed-care and doc-in-the-box structures.

"What about places that care for older people?" Joe's people asked. "What about skilled nursing facilities?"

"Yes, we don't have enough such places. It's a fast-growing industry."

As their customers expressed their needs and goals, KDA was ready to work with them and to help them expand in emergency medical as well as long-term-care situations.

Joe's business boomed with the construction of assisted living centers and a view toward long-term resident care for older citizens.

As one woman told Joe's staff, "I need a place for my mother to live. I can't put her in Florida, because I can't get down there often. I want her to be close by so I can care for her."

KDA made that drastic change to take advantage of the opportunities. That was 1995, and many businesspeople in Roswell, Georgia—just north of Atlanta—thought they were wrong. "We don't need those places here," more than one person remarked.

As of this writing, Roswell, Georgia, has five skilled nursing facilities. The business community already realizes they'll soon need others.

KDA didn't give up on banking and move totally into their new construction ventures. They listened to the bankers and were able to advise them, "Branch banking is going to change, but it won't die. We want to help you as you prepare for that change. We have created a whole division called site management."

KDA met with real estate specialists and asked, "What's going to change? What are the needs people are expressing about banking besides the Internet?"

"People like banks with people to talk to. But for that to work, we need to make branch banking simpler and more convenient. We need more branches, not less."

As Joe and his people pondered this situation, they came up with a simple solution—they could build branches inside large grocery stores. People could shop and bank at the same place. Joe's company contracted with a major grocery store chain to build branches inside their stores.

As a result of asking the right questions, Joe and his coworkers turned a shrinking industry into a growth industry, simply by looking at the threats and the challenges. For Joe, banking became a growth industry because he paid attention to consumer demands for convenience.

The next step was to ask: What can you do in a branch bank? and What kind of services do those customers need? This is ongoing, and who knows where the industry will go next?

I don't know and neither does anyone else. However, I'm sure Joe Hall and KDA will probably know before almost anyone else does.

This shows that when we approach customers with the idea of serving *their needs,* we too profit. Our customers need us to help them better see their future—something they often can't see for themselves.

If we're covenantal in that approach, we'll be able to partner with them. Together we can see change coming and adapt to it.

CHAPTER SIX

COVENANTING WITH CUSTOMERS
Five Significant Questions

How do you determine the customers who will covenant with you as compared to those who will not? Choosing the right customers is one of the factors for success that beyond-world-class companies stress.

That then leads us to ask how we go about choosing. In this chapter, I'm offering five questions we need to consider carefully.

1. If I Do Business with This Customer, Will They Violate My Principles?

Think principles here, because this first question doesn't refer to policies or products and services. Those three can change to meet needs. The real question is: Will working with this customer violate my principles in the way I treat my employees, suppliers, and other customers?

For example, at Black and White Technologies, a customer supplier came to Frank, the purchasing manager, and offered, "I can give you the best price on this if you'll share with me what some of the other suppliers are bidding. If you do, I'll make sure we beat their price and I'll make you look like a hero." Obviously, by violating the confidentiality of the bidding process he wanted to find out how low he had to bid.

"No, I can't do that," Frank responded. "If I show you their bids, I will be violating the covenant we have with them and that's not the way we do business."

The flabbergasted supplier shook his head. "You don't understand. I want to help you get this job by giving you the best price we can. I just need to know what I am up against."

"Let's turn it around. We wouldn't give your bid to one of your competitors, and we won't give their bid to you. That's not fair. If you want our business, make the best bid you can, and we'll decide fairly between all of them."

Angry and frustrated, the man stormed out of Frank's office.

That day Black and White Technologies might have been able to lower the cost of materials on a major project, but they acted covenantally. Frank turned his back on a potential great deal, but in doing so he maintained their covenantal principles.

Despite an angry retort from the customer supplier, Frank held his ground. "We will not do business with a noncovenantal supplier," had been his final words.

Another company got the job.

Frank knew he had done the right thing and never regretted making that decision.

That's not the end of the story. A few weeks later at the end of a meeting, various contractors sat around and spoke informally with each other. The man Frank had turned down grumbled to the others and told the story. "I tried to help him out by giving him the lowest price, but he wouldn't go along. He wouldn't even tell me what price I had to beat. He left good money on the table."

"You're kidding?" another asked. "Why would they act like that?" This conduct was common practice among contractors.

"Can you believe anyone being that stupid?" the angry man said. "I mean, I was ready to throw our business at them. They wouldn't show me anything. I could have saved them some serious dollars."

A very large general contractor who didn't engage in such practices listened to the complaints about the policy at Black and White Technologies. He asked a few questions. "You mean they have standards so high they would sacrifice profitability for principle?"

"Yeah, the dummies."

A few days later that questioning contractor called Trent Beighle, the president of Black and White, and said, "We've been awarded the contract on the municipal building in downtown Dayton. We want you to be our electrical contractor. We're not even putting it out for bid."

"We'd like to do it, but you're a union contractor," Trent said. "We're not union. Won't that cause you a lot of grief?"

"I want you anyway," he said. "I want you to do the design. From now on, Black and White Technologies is my electrical contractor. You come on board for the design process."

They talked for several minutes before a puzzled Trent asked him, "Why did you come to us? We've never done business with you before."

"I'll give you two reasons," the contractor offered. "Number one, I checked on Black and White Technologies. You guys do great work. Your history of solid work speaks for itself and you've been in business long enough that you're not going to fold up and fly away."

After Trent thanked him for that compliment, the contractor added, "But number two is a more important reason." He told Trent the story about the meeting of the contractors. "He was extremely angry at you for not opening that bid and allowing him to underbid his competitor. He swore at you as if you'd committed the worst crime in business. But you know what? That's when I decided you had the kind of integrity I admire.

Right then, I made up my mind that I wanted to do business with your company."

This true story shows the importance of refusing to work with companies that violate integrity. Every story may not have a happy ending like this one, but Trent Beighle knows that his people live by the principles they value. Frank certainly did the day he made the right decision.

There are even greater long-term benefits as we build strong relationships with suppliers, customers, and employees who do covenant with us. Because the nature of the marketplace is cyclical, volatile, and often hostile, companies are seeking as many constants as possible. One of those constants is long-term relationships based on mutual trust and respect.

The number of companies like Sklar Pepplar who made it through a tough time because of the commitment of customers, suppliers, and dedicated employees would be too long to print here; the number of companies that were abandoned because of their lack of integrity would be longer.

Integrity is like building a trust account. The bigger and more frequent the deposit, the greater the balance in a time of need. Quite possibly, integrity is the best insurance policy a leader can have.

DOES EVERYONE WIN?

2. Is This a Win-Win Situation?

In the previous scenario, this became more than a win-win situation, it became a triple-win situation. Black and White Technologies won, and their customer, the contractor, also won. So did the supplier to Black and White Technologies. No one had to lose for this success to take place.

Maybe I can explain it better if I take the opposite side of this. Let's say that Black and White Technologies wanted business so badly they violated their suppliers in order to get more business with their customers. By violate I mean suppose Frank read the other bid, knew what it could cost them to underbid, and then went to their suppliers and said, "We want that job. In order to get it, you have to cut your price to us. Then we can make the lower bid to guarantee that we get the contract."

Black and White Technologies might have won that job if they had asked that way. Or then again, would they have won, really?

The contractor would have won by getting the price he wanted—that's the only real winner in that version of the story. Black and White Technologies would have gotten the contract—and would have had to lower their profit to bring it about, which means they were not a true winner. They also would have stirred up bad feelings toward them, which again makes it a loss. But worse, the suppliers would have become the biggest losers. To get the order from Black and White Technologies they would have had to lower their prices, selling at prices below what they normally expected to receive.

Frank would then have given the usual line, "Look, work with us on this. I'll make it up to you on the next deal."

Maybe they would make it up. More likely, no makeup day ever arrives.

Because Black and White Technologies didn't play the win-lose game, everyone won. No one had to compromise, humiliate another, or do anything unethical. All three parties win in cove-nantal transactions.

I emphasize this point because some businesspeople think they win *only* if somebody loses. That may sound strange to many people, but such tactics are taught in conferences and workshops on negotiating. One well-known negotiator actually said, "You'd better make sure somebody loses or you don't really win."

That's not doing business covenantally. I wouldn't want to do business with anyone like that. Those who have that attitude need for somebody to take some sort of loss and don't feel good unless they make someone else feel bad. Such people are out there, but we don't have to do business with them. In fact, we don't want to because to them ethics and values mean nothing; all that matters is that they win. It's the spirit of competition stretched to really aberrant levels. So in the end, they don't really win.

BAD TANGO DANCERS

3. If They Are Going to Use You to Replace a Supplier, What Is Their History or Experience?

Changing suppliers happens all the time. Getting an offer from a new customer, especially one that could make our company a large profit, sounds good. But before we take that step, we need to ask: Is this what we call a bad tango dancer? When I use that term I mean they're dancing all over the floor, going from one partner to another, and they usually switch partners over credit issues or unscrupulous prices.

Bad tango dancers means *they* are looking for new suppliers because they haven't been good partners and no one dances with them very long. A common reason is because they haven't paid the old suppliers.

One of the first questions we need to ask—and make certain we get the correct answer—is, "How many suppliers have provided this product for you in the past five years?"

Once we get the answer, we then ask, "Who are they?"

These are reasonable questions, even if the proposed customer says, "That's confidential, I can't tell you."

The only sensible response then is to say, "Sorry, but we can't supply this product for you." By that answer, we're letting them know that we won't be mistreated or dance with them over bills that they either don't pay or delay paying.

I've asked that question enough times so I can almost guarantee that when a company refuses to give the answer, and if we check them out through Dunn and Bradstreet, we learn the real problems—slow pay, no pay, or some form of bad tango dancing.

The sad part is customers can just hop from one supplier to another. As long as they can get what they want, they don't seem concerned about violating their suppliers.

"There's always another company out there that wants to do business with us," one potential customer said to me years ago.

"It won't be us," I said. To myself, I added, You won't dance with me, because I want to be able to pay my bills and to take care of my suppliers and my other customers. No, I prefer to turn down such a dance invitation.

Some of the bad tango dangers are low-cost drivers. "There is so much competition for suppliers," they either say directly or imply, "that it doesn't matter if I drive the cost below the true cost, someone will take my offer."

These bad tango dancers come in and demand, "Sell it to us below your cost." It is unfortunate that some companies agree to dance, and by making such arrangements, they are eventually driven out of business. That happens—a lot—more often than we like to admit.

Here's a true example. A giant organization, which I'll call International Inc., came to a division of Ochs Industries (which is their real name). When International asked them for a price, Ochs provided it, and it was a good, fair price.

"We can get this for less," International said and named a competitor. The price International wanted was nearly 30 percent less than the Ochs' price.

"No one can sell at that price and make money," the Ochs representative insisted.

"This is the price we'll pay. Take it or leave it."

The two executives talked and Ochs did come down nearly 3 percent, but that obviously wasn't enough to satisfy them.

"We can do better," International said.

"There must be something wrong here," the Ochs man said. He argued extensively with the International rep because they were a big company and, ordinarily, a good company to do business with. The Ochs people refigured and worked on their bid and finally came back and said, "We cannot do this. We would lose money."

"We didn't think you could," the buyer confessed. He then named the company they had decided to buy from.

"But—but they're going out of business. Did you know that?"

"Yes, you're right. So we don't have to pay for their overhead. We're just paying the basic cost of materials and labor, and that's their price. They're in Chapter 11 and all they're trying to do right now is keep their doors open."

Ochs wisely lost the job. They were smart enough to realize that if they did business with unscrupulous companies that pushed them to sell below cost, eventually they too would be in Chapter 11.

WORSHIPING AT THE ALTAR OF VOLUME

4. Are They a Covenantal Company?

This question is for companies to consider when they're in contact with a potential customer. Do they worship at the sacred altar of sales volume? I've found this difficult to understand, but there are people who put so much emphasis on volume that they will do anything to get more sales. They don't always stop to ask what that means.

For too many, it's an equation that says increased volume means increased profits.

Maybe.

What happens if the volume outweighs the cost? What happens if we lose two cents on every product, but we tell ourselves we can make it up in volume of sales? That doesn't make sense. It's trying to say that if we lose enough money in sales per item we can recoup it through volume.

This kind of volume mentality kills companies, especially when they deal with a single major customer. Yet I've seen this happen hundreds of times. "We'll give you $10 million worth of sales," they say.

You know you're only going to lose a few cents on each sale, but how many cents will you lose on $10 million in sales?

It's not the fault of those who make this offer, because they're not violating any agreement. They're offering volume, and if we're foolish, we fall down and worship. But, in the long run, have we sold our souls to a false god? Is it really in our best interest to make such agreements?

To get the volume and the customers who will give you more volume—we must cut our cost. This means we may easily end up providing the product but at a loss. Then we try to fool ourselves into thinking that if we sell enough we'll make up for it. How is that possible?

Here's a delightful story I heard, and it expresses this idea well: A farmer sells watermelons, but he's not making any money. When his wife asks him why, he says, "I don't know. It costs me six dollars to grow the watermelons. When I take them to the market, I sell them all day long for five dollars. And they sell—I can sell every single one of them. You know what? I think I need a bigger truck so I can sell more."

He needs to stop selling watermelons for five dollars and stop thinking he can make it up in volume. He can't.

THE SECURITY OF DIVERSITY

5. Does This Customer Add Diversity to Our Customer Base?

By selling to this customer does it change the type of customers we have? Does it affect the size of the customer base?

Diversifying our customer base is actually covenantal. Think of what happens if all our customers look exactly the same. Let's say we're selling to the transportation industry. What happens when recession hits that industry? Will our company also go into recession?

We can avoid this serious pitfall by selling to a countercyclical industry.

For instance, let's say we supply products to Ford. Then we probably don't want to go to GM to provide more of the same product. If we're in the transportation industry, instead of looking at building cars, why don't we focus on companies that produce road-building equipment?

Here's another factor. If we study the automobile industry, we see that when their business goes up, down goes some of the business in the transportation industry. Conversely, when transportation goes up, the automobile industry goes down. Perhaps, along with Ford, it would do well for us to talk to the people at Caterpillar. Maybe we should talk to John Deere.

Here's one final consideration in the matter of diversity. As we consider the people we supply, it will help if we ask, "Where will this customer be in one year? In three years? In five? Will they be searching for another dance partner because of bad credit? Will they be buying at a low cost because two more competitors are going out of business and they can come in and buy their salvage?"

In this chapter, I've tried to focus on the future, but first we need to determine our covenantal responsibility to our customers and to our suppliers. It's important to stress that fact, and it works like this: If we provide a high-quality product or service that meets the needs of our customers, they will enter into a covenantal relationship with us. For example, they agree (covenant) that they will pay each of our invoices within 30 days. They will do that because of our covenantal relationship (our agreement is that we will stop supplying if they do not pay).

Yet it's more than billing and paying. Because of the now-existing and trusted relationship, they'll give us information we can use to help them increase their business and profitability. We can call this a matter of trust or ethical practices, but if we act covenantly and they respond in the same manner, we have made an informal partnership. They'll welcome our help now and will continue to ask for it in the future.

By contrast, I could easily point out many large, abusive corporations. They don't act covenantly, and they exploit the relationship by trying to take advantage of their suppliers. As I've already noted, they will use the price given by one supplier to go to the competitor and ask them to underbid.

In later chapters, I'll provide examples of what happens when companies resort to noncovenantal practices.

LEARNING THE HARD WAY

If we want to be a beyond-world-class company, we begin by making clear covenants with the companies with whom we do business. We make ourselves responsible and hold them responsible if they violate the covenant. Too often companies are so happy to get an order, especially if it's a big one, they ignore their ethical responsibilities.

Part of being covenantal is for our company to live up to our end of every agreement we make, explicitly or implicitly. If we do, we can expect our customers and suppliers to do the same.

If they fail to uphold their end of the covenant, we stop doing business with them. It's really that simple, but we may need to teach our customers what we expect of them and explain what they can expect of us. If we do our best to live up to our promises, we can expect the same from them.

Once we decide on our company's covenantal responsibility to our suppliers and customers, it's not a secret we hide in the company vault. Our next responsibility is to communicate and to teach these principles throughout the organization and even across the industry.

We have to make certain that we don't allow anyone in our organization to be unclear about what we're asking them to do. For instance, it's important for us not to ask our organization or any employees to set goals and objectives they don't understand. It is our responsibility to say something like, "Covenantally, this is what we're going to do on behalf of that customer."

Here's an example of how this works. The largest customer of Jim Nicklas, CEO at Greencastle Metal Works, was a company that, to protect the guilty, we'll refer to as TRI. When Jim met with their executives, he had the right answers and was ready to align himself with them. His only concern was that TRI was his largest customer.

If Greencastle put all of its efforts into a relationship that wasn't mutual, they would be the losers. Jim got an okay with his board and moved forward because they were tracking positively in the right industry at the right time. All the internal decisions coming from the top people at TRI indicated that they could and would enter into a covenantal partnership.

We advised Jim, "If TRI is willing to work with you as you help them realize future growth, and if you're going to put your company's money into this, get it in writing."

Jim tried, but they never would give him a contract. They always had excuses or made promises, but they never gave him anything that was signed. Greencastle unwisely entered into an expensive undertaking—a million-dollar investment—all on a handshake.

Hindsight would have demanded Jim Nicklas to say to TRI, "I want you to understand that we're totally behind you. All we need is a supplier contract agreement."

I do want to point out that despite his personal reservations, the board advised Jim to go ahead, so he didn't make this agreement by himself. Consequently, Greencastle invested heavily in the future of TRI.

Jim conducted surveys, asked questions, and talked to many people in the TRI organization about their future. He saw they had the ability to move into the international arena and they were on a growth track for at least the next ten years. To grow effectively, they would need to outsource to companies, such as Greencastle Metal Works. (Many companies contract with individuals and companies for services. The business world has done this for years with their needs for printing, advertising, and engineering. Now they also are contracting with companies for accounting, contract manufacturing, marketing, technology, and even research and development.)

TRI manufactures high-lift and other construction equipment. Greencastle would build steel chassis for the engines and the hydraulics and the wheels that went into their forklifts. Representatives from Greencastle carefully studied what they needed to do. Their covenantal responsibility was to hire staff and to be able to do the things needed to provide the products. One of the things they did was agree to a rigid production schedule.

In order for Greencastle to grow, they had to spend money and they performed everything as they had promised.

Jim had seen the future of TRI clearly. He saw it because he and his engineering group, as well as other staff members, went to TRI and did the necessary research, asked the right questions, and invested many hours and a lot of money to guide TRI toward the right steps for them to take.

As part of that objective, Jim determined his covenantal responsibility to them and met with their executives. "You're outsourcing and you're going to be doing more of that during the next ten years. Here's what Greencastle can do for you."

Everything Greencastle suggested was first-class and practical. A high level of excitement developed between the two organizations.

There was only one problem: Jim Nicklas and Greencastle Metal Works was a covenantal company; TRI wasn't.

TRI violated their end of the verbal contract.

Jim and his people had shown TRI how to make their product more efficiently. One day, an executive of TRI told them, "We've had a slowdown in orders, and we need to pull some of the work you were doing back in-house."

Within 30 days, TRI took away about 30 percent of Greencastle's business. That was quite a blow because they had purchased material, designed equipment, and hired people to meet the needs of TRI for anticipated long-term business. Greencastle went from a highly successful business to a company that was barely hanging on.

Within six months, TRI took away another 30 percent of their business. When Jim protested, they did relent and returned about 20 percent of it. Even so, TRI constantly changed their policies, and Greencastle had no idea what they would do next.

"They played me like a yo-yo," Jim said later. "Up and down, and up and down."

For several months, Greencastle stayed with TRI and suffered the indignity. Finally, their board met and decided, "We have chosen to be a covenantal company. TRI is not covenantal. We've tried to work ethically with them, and they have violated every agreement we have made. We will no longer do business with them."

How does this true story end? Jim Nicklas wholeheartedly agreed with the board and went to the top officials of TRI and told them, "We are not operating this way with you any longer.

We'll go out of business before we do this again. If we continue the way things are going, you'll put us out of business anyway." He also let them know that Greencastle had lived up to their agreements and from now on they would do business only with covenantal companies.

He received no concessions from TRI; the relationship was broken.

The next several months were extremely difficult for Greencastle, but they had made their decision to act covenantally, and they stuck with it. From that time on, Greencastle worked only with those customers whom they felt would respond ethically. Jim Nicklas assumed responsibility to ensure that their dealings with every supplier and every customer would promote the covenant relationship.

The company survived. Within a few months, they became profitable again.

Two years later, can you guess who came calling on Greencastle to do business with them?

TRI contacted Jim Nicklas and told him they wanted to work with them. "What we did to you wasn't fair," they agreed. "Our actions lacked integrity. We didn't really see it from your perspective." They promised to throw $20 million worth of business to Greencastle.

"We can do that. We have the capacity and we know where you're going," Jim responded. But that wasn't the end of the conversation. Jim explained that he would be their supplier *only* if they made a covenantal agreement in writing so he could be certain they wouldn't violate it.

They protested and didn't want to sign anything.

"In the past, your deeds haven't lined up with your words," he said calmly. "I want a contract."

"We never do that. We can't do that . . ."

"Then we can't work together," Jim said. "I want your promises and agreements to be written down very clearly, and especially I want the contract to state what you will suffer if you violate that covenant."

"What do you mean by what we will suffer?"

"If you throw $20 million worth of business our way, I need a certain amount of time to do things, such as buy new equipment and go through a hiring process. But I'm not going to go through that again and then have you bail out and we end up with a heavy financial loss. If you pull out after you agree, you will pay anyway."

TRI didn't know how to treat a supplier covenantally. Greencastle took a serious risk. "Our integrity is worth more than twenty million dollars," Jim said.

Most people would have said, "Okay, TRI learned from that experience." TRI said they had and wouldn't do it again, but they refused to put anything in writing.

Jim still wouldn't budge. "Before we can do business again I need to know that you will fulfill your part of the covenantal commitment. We have proven faithful in our part. I think your future is good, but I won't let you violate my covenant with my employees because I accept your word."

When I learned about that, I congratulated Jim and his people. They had become a beyond-world-class company by their willingness to lose millions of dollars of potential orders because they weren't willing to ramp up, hire, and train people they might not be able to keep employed if TRI resorted to their normal business practices. They had chosen to be ethical and treat their own suppliers and employees with respect.

One of Greencastle's competitors might easily have given in and justified that decision by saying, "Hey, it's only short term. It looks good, and we can make more money."

Jim and Greencastle are adamant. "We live by a covenant and our customers also will live by that covenant or we don't do business together."

True to their way of operating, as TRI's business slowed, they again pulled all their operations away from Greencastle.

Fortunately for Jim, his principles have paid off. He replaced the TRI business with more profitable business from a covenantal supplier willing to develop a true, long-term partnership.

At the time of this writing, I keep asking myself, Will the management principles of TRI change? I don't know. I know right now they are looking at themselves and facing up to some of their unethical behavior. What about TRI executives? Will they ever understand the negative impact of their actions? It will happen only when the leaders begin to see the direct relationship between how they treat their suppliers and how they treat their customers.

Maybe they'll catch on and become a company of integrity.

I hope so.

CHAPTER SEVEN

BEYOND MARKETING 101
Continuous Solutions Development

Most companies have what I call the Marketing 101 approach when it comes to asking questions. They look to the marketing department as the people who support sales by asking buyers a few questions. They also create printed material, four-color brochures, and other attractive literature. They're responsible for promotion and advertising, so they're always thinking of ways to promote to a buyer.

They're faced with one constant issue: How can we increase our sales volume? The pressure is on them to produce more sales, and they usually work hard at it, but they're not solving problems. They may think they are, but most of the time they're still doing Marketing 101.

Marketing 101 *is* vital, but that's the small, easy part. If we want to go on to the next level, and all progressive companies do, what's next for them? If I gave this a college course name, I'd call it Advanced Strategic Marketing 404. This course would start by saying we have to look beyond merely more sales and ask ourselves, What happens after the sale? What lies ahead for us and for our customers and suppliers?

If we focus on Advanced Marketing, it means that we develop solutions—continuously—and we don't just do hasty searches. We don't scurry for easy, expedient answers as each problem arises. In fact, if we have our principles in place, we're ready for those problems before they arise.

First, however, we have to know whether we're organized to work from business-to-business solutions (B2B) or business-to-consumer solutions (B2C). How we proceed makes a tremendous difference.

If it's B2C solutions, we need solid market research on consumer behavior. A number of firms can do that for us. But if our customers are B2B, we need to understand that they've probably gotten access to research that we need in order to help them. Today we can pull a lot of that information off the Internet.

We can do our own research and find what we need to know. Some people are amazed to learn how many companies don't do research and do nothing to access research that's already been done and is easily available.

If we know how to find the research to use for their benefit, we add enormous tactical value to the situation. If it's a B2B approach, our job is easier, because we go to the business itself and do the strategic research with them. That is, we offer to help them.

For example, we went in to do an assessment at S.D. Myers, a provider of electrical transformer services. Prior to our first meeting with them, we researched their customers on the Internet. By reviewing current industry publications, we rapidly determined the key industry issues and developed our questions based on that analysis. We were later able to go through 32 interviews for them with an incredible base of knowledge that made us look as if we really understood the issues.

What was remarkable—and remember, we are not in this industry and this company is one of the best at what they do—is that we were able to recognize some significant opportunities that an entire sales and marketing team of 25 to 30 people had not been aware of. We did our research with their current and future customer base. In so doing, we learned what was happening to their customers' customers. The outcome was significant.

We were able to help them establish a second company built around the concept of solutions. The first company continues to provide services as they've always done. The second company provides solutions, and this allows them to sell more of their services, become more important to their customers, develop new services that customers need, and position themselves within their customer base at a completely different level than where they've been in the past.

REVERSE ENGINEERING

Even more important, after less than six hours of Internet research at Corporate Development Institute (CDI), we were able to show them these answers. Why could we do that and they couldn't?

Of course, they could have done the same thing, but they had become so busy conducting daily business and, like most companies, they were bound to unexpressed "we've-always-done-it-that-way" thinking. No one had stopped to engage in research or decide what they needed to know to move forward.

Because we had no knowledge to begin with, we had to start in the future and work backward. We were more open to seeing it from the standpoint of their customers' future than they were. Again, they weren't different from most other companies.

Japan used the principle of reverse engineering during the Korean war to develop an industrial production capability that built their country into an economic powerhouse. This concept, brought about because of our lack of trust and cooperation, actually served the Japanese well.

Most of the large equipment refurbishing or rebuilding done during the Korean War took place in Japan because of their capacity and proximity. Unfortunately, when we sent them a tank to rebuild, we failed to give them the vital information, the how-to manual. Being resourceful, and hungry, they took the tank apart and reverse engineered it, building up their knowledge base as they went.

What happened when the tanks returned to Korea? They lasted longer, performed better, and were generally improved versions of the original. Obviously, in the course of reverse engineering we learn what not to do as well as what we must do to bring about a better product, service, or solution.

In much the same way, we must "re-engineer" our customers' needs by starting with their future and working backward. Information availability is at an all-time high, so there is no excuse for not doing the homework.

The power of the Internet to research customer and industry information is well known, but I'm amazed at how seldom companies use it to research their customers, their customers' competitors, and their customers' customers.

When we began to work with S.D. Myers, there were two specific places we gathered our information—their own Web sites and the sites of their competitors. It's amazing how much good information we were able to find. The real source of our information, however, came from industry and trade association Web sites, which feature articles written on related subjects that we could easily find and quickly catalogue.

MARKETING MATRIX

As simple as this may sound, the first two factors are basic. First, we need to be quite clear whether our business is structured for B2B or B2C. The second factor in Advanced Strategic Marketing is research analysis. That is, we organize how we're going to talk to our customers. We need to develop what I call the customer *matrix*—an idea-filter situation within which something originates or develops. We develop an environment conducive to solutions by starting with questions that take us to the point where a solution is visible. It is much like taking someone to the edge of the Grand Canyon and then asking, "What do you see?" Too often we stay at the hotel and stare at pictures when we ought to be on the front lines of change and opportunity.

We start to create the matrix when we ask, "Who has answers to the questions I'm going to ask?"

Seldom will the person with answers be the buyer. But we need to be very careful here and think of the problem it can create if we bypass those who don't have the answers we seek. The approach differs when we try to work with an existing customer as opposed to an attempt to sell into a potential customer.

Consider our approach to a potential customer. If we go in selling the concepts of covenant and continuous solutions all at once, we will probably fail miserably. But we do have to get to the right people. If we enlist the buyer as a vital team member, we use an existing customer as a potential model for referral. Once they begin to develop the contact list, we know we're in.

For current customers, the fact that we have been developing a covenant relationship will be the door opener with buyers already committed to a more involved partnership. In either case, we're really using the covenant relationship and the desire to serve our customers better by developing solutions to position ourselves. Once the concept is sold, the rest is easy.

Here's another thing to consider: If it's a perspective customer, be aware that the company has already erected all kinds of barriers to keep out people like us. Too many salespeople have used every trick in the book to bypass the system so most companies have built in protective measures. I know. We have them at CDI.

Instead of trying to tear down the walls, we need to create that matrix and march past those barriers. That is, we need to create the atmosphere where *they* want our solutions. Great solutions always start with great questions.

The first question is: How do I get in a position to talk with representatives of that company?

Depending on the industry, the people responsible for strategy tend to be the people open to solutions. The size of the company dictates whether that is the CEO, COO, CFO, or at the vice-president level. Don't assume that title designates strategic positioning. We have to dig to find out who they are. Here's my suggestion. It's fine to approach the buyer if we do it correctly. If we go to the buyer and recognize that person as part of a *team*, not as someone to push past, then we ask, "Can you help me? We want to do a strategic research analysis with your company. We want to sell to you, but we want to be sure we have the necessary information and that we're able to produce what you need."

This attitude is the matrix and it's a critical step. That will lead us to the answer to our next question: From whom does the buyer get approval? One way is to find out *from the buyer* who has the authority to say no. Enlist the buyer as our partner, someone we need (and we do need the buyer!), and as a person who can help us help her company. If the buyer becomes our partner, she can help us get to the people who can say yes.

But if we create the matrix—the atmosphere—of trust and mutuality with those on the bottom rungs of the ladder, they will eagerly lead us up the ladder themselves.

"Yes, but how will I convince these people to be part of this process?" is a natural question.

The easiest, most natural way, and the one that has worked incredibly well, is to say, "We want to do a strategic market analysis for you." That's honest and it's to the point. The emphasis is on the last two words: *for you.* "We'd like to do this for you, and we'll give you the results from our surveys. This is a service. We hope the end result will be that we'll receive business from you, but we also recognize this as a chance we're taking. You are under no obligation, no matter how helpful our material may be."

We also need to remind ourselves that this is exactly what we mean and accept the consequences if they like the data but don't want our services. Yet, I can't think of a single instance when an approach like this did not result in a positive outcome. Sometimes it was merely a door opener, but eventually the customer appreciated the information and approach.

Many buyers will see this as helping them and their company. They then become eager to set up a meeting. This happens all the time. It works and it will continue to work as long as they stay part of the picture *and know that they're controlling it internally.* Expect—even urge—them to control the situation and they will benefit from this. That's why this approach is so appealing—they gain.

Another aspect is that today there is an immense amount of pressure on buyers to solve problems—and that pressure entails more than buying cheaply. If the buyer we're talking to has only one objective—to buy everything at the lowest price and increase its profit margin—we probably don't want to work with that company anyway, because this indicates it's not a covenantal company.

As I've shown in previous chapters, noncovenantal organizations often push us to lower our prices. This is something they do later, at a time when we're the most vulnerable to them. Instead, we want to focus on companies where we have a future together. When we find covenantal customers, they're ones that will want our help.

When we start talking about Advanced Strategic Marketing, our goal is to work toward solutions that are two generations ahead. That is, we don't want to solve only their immediate problems but we want to enable them to solve the problems they haven't yet seen, and even go beyond that.

At the same time we're helping them, we want to enable them to help *their* customers. Sometimes buyers and lower-level people have trouble seeing ahead or thinking of their customers' customers. We arrive on the scene to raise their consciousness level. We want to reach people who are thinking of their customers' customers.

This isn't as discouraging as it may sound. The best way to make this happen is for us to have done research on their customers' customers and be able to say truthfully, "We've done some research and this is the information we have come up with."

FORTRESS 2000

Here's another example of how this works. Earlier, I talked about the work we did with the J. Smith Lanier Company (JSL), an insurance company, which is a customer-based organization. Before we met, however, I did my research and learned some of the pressures they were under. My role was to sell our service to the seven people who represented JSL.

Rather than just trying to sell service, I asked them several hard questions. Once I got them thinking, I presented the information I had learned from my research. I'd like to point out that my research was reliable—no guesswork or made-up information. That also is part of our integrity—to present the truth at all times.

As I made my presentation and told the JSL representatives about the problems and pressures they faced, I could see from their reactions that several questions went through their minds: How does he know this? Where did he get all this information? He's not even in this industry, so how could he have information that even we don't have?

When I finished, two of their representatives verified that my research was accurate. "I read that myself," one of them said.

Not only did I look credible, but I also helped those two executives look more credible to their peers. Even though I was the outsider, without trying to be secretive or sound superior, I told them where I had gotten my information. Why not? I had nothing to hide.

In presenting such research, our purpose isn't to show that we're superior. Our purpose is to help our client. Thus, one of the main things we do when using this avenue for research is to plan what it is we are trying to find out. If we had limited our research sources, we would have found out only what they already knew and would never have seen the potential in knowing what they didn't know.

Once they realized I had come prepared, I moved forward and asked them six specific questions about their industry. They didn't know all the answers—and I knew they wouldn't—but they recognized that I knew the questions they needed to grapple with. From then on, we were able to work together.

A little later, one of them lamented, "Even with the answers, we don't know how to take advantage of what you're telling us. If you can perceive something we don't know on how to apply this, we want you to show us."

I affirmed that they still had to do all the things involved in Marketing 101, including such simple tasks as advertising and putting together brochures. "It's after Marketing 101 that you start becoming a solutions company. When that happens, you move toward *continuous* solutions development. How can you help your customers develop new solutions if you don't understand the industries they're in? You have to understand what they do on behalf of their customers. To get that information, you have to do the research—you can't avoid that step. If you're willing to put time and effort into learning what they need, you can become much more valuable to customers. You don't just sell them once, but you become a covenantal customer—usually for life."

I wanted the JSL executives to realize that when they partner with their clients—and this happens only when they fully understand their customers' needs and work toward solving them together—the relationship changes. Between them, a level of trust develops and because of that, they enjoy working together. There isn't that constant haggling over price and an element of trying to win at the other's expense.

In making my final presentation to JSL's executive leadership, I introduced a competitive product that was being offered in their market area, a product I called Fortress 2000. As I shared the components of Fortress 2000, the customers it was being marketed toward and the specifics of implementation, I could sense a change in the tone of the meeting.

What I presented was a potential threat to them, because it would have been a real solution to their client needs. The product would provide a complete risk-management fortress around each targeted client.

At one point, a senior vice president leaned over to the COO and said, "I'll bet it's Aon." (That was a larger, aggressive competitor.)

When I finished and had their attention, I asked, "I imagine you would like to know who it is that's about to rock your world?" They nodded.

When I flipped to the last slide, they saw *Alan M. Ross* written on the page. I said, "I have no experience in this industry, but if I can create a program and a solution that made most of you adjust your chairs and take a deep breath, why can't you? Don't wait for the competition to develop the solution. You do it first and give them fits."

Fortress 2000 is in the third year of implementation. J. Smith Lanier is blowing away the competition. All it took was setting up the matrix, asking the right people the right questions, and then coming up with a likely solution to clear problems. It is really all about working and thinking smart, thinking ahead, and understanding that change brings opportunities.

SEEING FROM A DIFFERENT PERSPECTIVE

Here are two examples of how a search for continuous solutions development functions.

1. S.D. Myers

I've already referred to the merger of S.D. Myers and SunOhio (see Chapter 4), the transformer consultants that serve industrial customers in small utilities in electrical transformers. To a greater extent than anyone else in the nation, they probably know more about electrical transformers, taking the pollutant PCB out of them, and maintaining them. They were already doing a good job.

I was aware that the sales and marketing people, pushed at what they were already doing, had no extra time to figure out where S.D. Myers was going in the future.

We decided to start by focusing on their customers. Working with their sales and marketing department, we helped them to develop the approach of continuous solutions development. That is, they sought solutions long before they became aware of encroaching problems.

First, we asked all the sales and marketing managers and salespeople to spend two days doing research with their customers. But before we sent them out to do the research, we asked for their own answers.

"What is your customers' number one concern?" we asked.

"Lower prices," the sales and marketing staff answered. "If they can get lower prices for our services, they'll be more interested in signing on with us."

"What do you think is the second major concern?"

"They want high quality."

"What's the third?" I asked.

"They want flexibility. They want us to get there when they need us and not just when we can get around to it." They explained that sometimes their customers had to shut down a plant in order to install the transformers. That required flexibility to fit into the schedule of the factory.

After the two days, they returned with the results of their questionnaires. To their amazement, they learned that their customers' first concern was *time*. The people they interviewed had already seen cutbacks in the company and in the industry. Some of them were already doing the job formerly done by two or even three people. Because of time pressures, they couldn't finish all the priorities they had in front of them.

Number two for the customers, was *reliability*. Because of the time factor, when something didn't stay fixed, it became a serious issue. If they couldn't factor in reliability, it cost them twice as much time to repair—time they didn't have.

Third was *cost;* fourth was *quality*.

As we discussed this, one of the S.D. Myers executives finally saw the light. "Wait a minute! We're one of their biggest time wasters. We have five divisions and that means we have five salesmen calling on every customer."

Because the time pressures placed on the buyers of their service was the number one issue, S.D. Myers reorganized the sales efforts to minimize the time involved with transformer issues. They called it a "Covenant with Customers."

Of course, we liked that at CDI.

The second issue, reliability, is the strength of the S.D. Myers Company—that's what they're best at. Unfortunately, in the past they hadn't emphasized this as much as they needed to. That is, instead of emphasizing reliability, it was merely something they either mentioned in passing or took for granted that everyone knew.

We put them firmly on to the concept of one-stop shopping for their customers. "We can save you time," they were able to say. "You don't have to put this stuff to five bids. It's just one bid.

You already know we're the best and most reliable, and we'd like to have more of your business." They focused on their strength and coupled it with the others' needs. "We've just solved your problem," they said.

Something else that helped S.D. Myers. was that they distinguished between their industrial customers and smaller utilities and contractors. That is, they didn't offer the same answers to smaller companies as they did to larger utilities. That meant they put different *policies* into effect, but they remained constant in their *principles*.

While we were helping them to figure out how to work with large corporations, one of their salespeople commented, "I wish we would get together with the contractors and all these other people we sell to and then come up with one overall policy."

They decided to sit down with former competitors and ask, "What if we came together and set up standards and guidelines? All we'd have to do is line up a few of them, and if we work together in marketing to the large utility companies, we'll all hit a home run."

"We'll find that our former competitors," another said, "have become our allies."

S.D. Myers made significant changes in the way they did business, and it all came about when they put the customer in the middle. No matter how good any company is, unless the customer is in the middle, they are not doing Advanced Strategic Marketing 404. The day they began to change into a beyond-world-class company was the day they developed a covenant with their customers.

SEEING A DIFFERENT FUTURE

2. Beach Mold and Tool

Beach Mold and Tool is a plastic ejection molding dye and manufacturer. They make plastic products and their electronics industry division includes customers such as Sony, as well as larger telephone and computer companies. In fact, they made plastic cases for laptops for one of the top producers in the country. Because there's so much plastic in the telecommunications and electronics industry, they had gone after that end of the business, got a lot of it, and were good at what they did.

The company created an advanced strategic marketing approach and went to some of their top customers and said, "We're the best at what we do. We want to bid on more of your business because we do more and more of what you need."

Those companies, already good customers, were willing to look at Beach's other services and products.

Actually, they did this themselves and we use it as a model. Beach Mold and Tool has a powerful strategic marketing plan based on developing solutions for their clients. Many of their clients had developed a position called Commodity Manager, who was responsible for all commodity purchases and contract manufacturing agreements.

Their customer was looking for solutions to the sheer number of commodity parts they had to purchase and assemble. Beach Mold and Tool decided to offer an integrated product that included not only the plastic components, but also offered the metal components and assembly. It was a solution, yet it continuously evolves.

Whenever Beach Mold and Tool is able to integrate more into the product, they partner with existing suppliers, taking the responsibility off of the customer. It is only a matter of time before Bill Beach adds the final solution to their services, which will be the electronic components themselves.

From a simple plastic mold to an integrated manufactured solution; that is the power of continuous solutions development. It can make the difference between a world-class company and one that is beyond world class.

What lies ahead for Beach Mold and Tool? To move forward effectively, we pointed out that they have to become a global organization.

"How can we become global?" they asked. Once they knew the question, they went to work to find the solution. "What is it you need?" is the first question Beach asked customers. Then they listened carefully to the answers.

Because of that strategy alone—and there were others—they have been able to stay ahead of customer needs. Beach Mold and Tool will soon become a large electronics integrator, and that means they'll make virtually everyone's computer, including putting the electronics in the laptops.

That's quite a stretch when we realize that they began simply as a plastics manufacturer.

What would happen if Beach Mold and Tool didn't surge forward like that? Somebody else would have. The electronics people would get the work or the metal people would take it on—some company would have caught on to the need for an integrated product.

Beach Mold and Tool just got there first.

They're the company that did it and the industry is being changed as a result. Beach Mold and Tool changed, and they have since become an international organization. In the process, they said to the computer maker, "You can't afford to buy from three sources and then assemble everything. You need one source, and we can be that source."

The next step in the advancing of Beach Mold and Tool is in cabinetry for the plastic and the metal. Who knows where they'll go after that?

To take a more obvious example, where did Apple get the idea for their translucent machines? It came from a plastics manufacturer who did some research and concluded, "People would love to see the inside of this thing. Translucence and colors are what's big with Gen Xers."

Apple, almost out of business, had enough sense to listen to the research. The laptop is just plastic yellow or green, but the new design has hit a home run for Apple.

This is what we mean by continuous solutions.

CHAPTER EIGHT

THE MODEL OF A SOLUTION

Below is a graph that I call the solution scale. We can actually create these with every single product. We'll give the generic one and then we'll give examples of it.

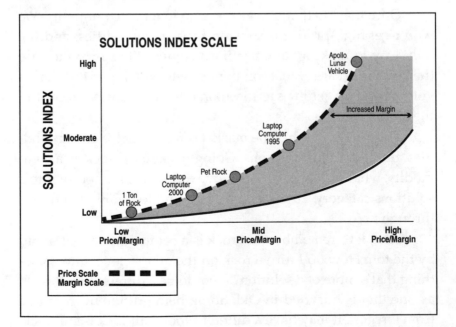

SOLUTIONS INDEX SCALE

Here's the point I want to make: When we operate on the commodities scale, we'll always stay down at the low end of the price scale. Let's take a specific example and show how we can raise that price and the profit.

Let's use one company that mines rock. That means they're in the quarry business. Their product is rock and they sell it as a commodity on a per-ton basis.

How can we make that rock more of a solution?

If the quarry people can answer that, their selling price will increase. But more important, their profit margin will also increase.

I want to drive home the point that commodities always have the lowest profit margins because, by nature, they're simply commodities and we can't protect them. Air, for instance, is air. Anyone call sell air. Water is another commodity. People do sell water more expensively than others and how do they do it? They brand-name their product and move it into being a solution product. They oxygenate it, ozone it, distill it, purify it, or find a way to show that it's good for our health.

Once they do that, the water is no longer a commodity. We won't get high-profit margins on those commodities, and the only way to make a large profit on commodities is to increase the volume of sales. Most companies who worship at the altar of volume end up getting sacrificed on it by the giants who control the altar.

This points out that the market offers no help for commodities, but it does for solutions. Going back to the rock as a commodity, what we have to do is move our rock commodity into a solutions category. To do this, we're going to follow two things through here.

First, let's remember that rock is a commodity and it's sold by the ton. How do I turn a rock on the quarry level into something that's more of a solution? It could be a different rock, such as one that is quarried in Oklahoma being different from one from Oregon. It may have a different look, but rock is still rock.

People will seldom pay more just because it came from Oklahoma or Oregon or anywhere else.

But let's say I take that rock for which I now pay $100 a ton—the commodity price. Somebody comes along and says to me, "I want to sell you my rock. I know you're paying $100, but my rock is better so my asking price is $110 a ton."

"Why is your rock better?"

"Well, it just is." They may give the location it came from or claim to have washed it three extra times or to have used a different drilling process. None of that matters because the product stays essentially the same.

"No, that's not true that your rock is better," I say. "So it's still $100 a ton. I can get it for that price, but if you'll lower your price to $95 I'll do business with you."

When that happens, the contractor is competing only with price.

But suppose the quarry owner talks with one of their current customers and asks, "When you buy rock, what are you going to use it for?" (Notice, this is a question that focuses on the customer's needs.)

"We use it to make driveways."

"What do you do with the rock when we send it to you?"

"We take it to a pulverizing machine and turn it into crushed rock and then we use it on the driveways."

"Is that expensive for you?"

"You bet it is. We've got to crush it one size for one driveway, and then a few days later, we crush it at a different texture for another style driveway. Every job doesn't call for the same size rock."

"What if I pulverized the rock and delivered it as crushed rock?"

"That'd be good and would help us."

"If I did that, I'd charge you $125 a ton for the finished product for you to use."

A quick calculation by the contractor gets a warm smile and a nod. "Yes, that would save us money as well as a lot of time."

If that happens, I have just gotten an additional $25 for rock. It will cost me a little more money to do it, but I'll earn a higher profit by putting it through a crusher.

That's a start. But crushed rock is still somewhat commoditized. So we ask the next question. "How do you put down the crushed rock?"

"We haul it in trucks. They dump it and then we hire laborers to spread it out."

"What if I had a machine that would spread the crushed rock as the truck dumped it? That way you'd have very little labor. Would that be helpful to you?"

"Of course! That would save us a lot of money in labor costs."

"I'll invest in such a machine so that I can deliver and lay down your crushed rock for $175 a ton. After that, you'll have minor labor costs."

If the contractor agrees, I've increased my profits immensely—and the rock has now become more than just a commodity.

We're now moving toward solutions and we're not stopping yet. Once that's in place, we ask, "Do you have any special needs?"

"Whenever we deal with government jobs, the rock has to be a specific size. For some reason, the government contracts state the specific size they want."

"Well, for a specialized rock run, my price will be $185, and again, it's laid for you."

"That will work for us."

This is a simplistic example, but it shows that I'm beginning to build up a solution rather than simply offering a commodity.

We might even stretch this further. Suppose I make a small wooden box and ask contractors, "Do you have a hard time buying a gift for your customers?" When they say yes, I answer, "I've got something that may work for you. We take one of our rocks, polish it, and put it in a box on a little nest of blue velvet, with a short note. We now call that polished rock a 'pet rock.' For each of these gift boxes, I would charge you only $14.95."

One company actually offered this service, and customers bought thousands of those pet rocks.

No matter how they dressed up stones and put them into beautiful boxes, it was still rock that sold for $100 a ton. When customers bought the same stone in the form of a pet rock, it sold for nearly $100,000 a ton.

What does all of this mean? It means we have to take the commodity and move it into products that provide solutions for businesses. When we do that, we are in the area of finding continuous solutions.

FROM CHICKENS TO CHICKEN WASTE

I want to tell you about one such company that has been extremely successful in finding continuous solutions. It is Boester Industries of Vancouver, Canada. When we first worked with them, they had a well-run business in which they ground and delivered mulch. They operated strictly at the commodity level.

How could Bill Boester grow his business by developing solutions? He looked for new, specialized uses for his products. One new industry was the chicken industry, because they would use his finely ground mulch to line the coops. Once the chickens grew and were removed, the soiled mulch was removed and a new layer put down.

While developing this business, Boester began to offer hauling services, using their existing tractors to hook up to chicken haulers. Everything seemed to be going along fine until their biggest customer decided to change the way they removed the chickens. With the change came new equipment and Bill was left with a fleet of trucks and a lot of soiled chicken mulch.

Bill did not give up on finding solutions. Because he had developed relationships in the chicken-processing industry, he spent time asking the right people the right questions, such as, "What is your biggest transportation headache?"

"Chicken waste," they said. New environmental standards were making it difficult for processors to eliminate the waste. It was likely that the problem would only get worse.

Guess who is now in the waste management business, which is a very profitable and growing industry? Bill Boester is building a company that is beyond world class in an industry that most of us would never dream possible.

The opportunities for developing high-margin solutions are all around us.

WWW.RADIO.COM

Here's a second scenario of moving from commodity to continuous solution. We had a three-day meeting in Texas with a large group of business owners, including a radio station in Brownsville, Texas. As we did with other companies, we stressed building covenants with customers and creating solutions.

"That's good for everybody else," explained one of the executives, "but it won't work for us. We're a religious radio station in a narrowly defined market. We have only a certain number of customers." In the period we met together, we also learned that some of that limited supply of customers didn't pay their bills well.

"We've sold advertising space to everyone we can. Not only do we have churches, but also lawyers, banks, stores, tax experts, chiropractors, and even service organizations."

"Why don't you ask them some questions?" we asked.

In fact, our company, Corporate Development Institute (CDI), did just that for them. One customer was a financial planner whom we asked, "What's happening with you and your advertising? You're paying the radio station to advertise for you and what are you getting in return?"

"Not as much business as we used to. It's getting much more difficult to promote and advertise," he said. "It's also getting difficult for me to maintain relationships with my customers."

As we talked, he moaned that his competitors were opening Web sites, "That's new to me, and I don't know what else to do but to set up a Web page as well." He said that he had cut back on his radio advertising because he was allocating part of the advertising budget to cope with the Web crisis.

As I listened, the proverbial light went on, and I knew the direction to go. I asked the radio station owner, "What does this problem have to do with your station?"

"I don't see the connection," he said, not sure of where I was going.

"How many other customers do you think are worried about this Web thing?" I asked.

"A lot. Maybe most of them."

"How much would it cost for you to get a Web design engineer? Then you could offer this as a solution to charter customers."

"What do you mean by charter customers?"

"I mean those who advertise over the course of the year. You could create and maintain a Web site for them. It would be your Web site with your station's call numbers on it. Listeners can come to your site and all your advertisers will be listed there. Instead of hearing a dozen ads every day with a dot-com address for each, they'll hear only one—and that one will be your station's."

He liked the idea.

"Your Web site will become the radio yellow pages for all of your customers. Can you do that cheaper than they could each do it individually?"

He nodded.

"You can offer this as a service."

One of the people present during this discussion was a man who owned an accounting firm. Immediately he asked, "How much would you charge me?"

Before the station had launched the Web site, the owner already had his first customer!

Less than a year later, the station had their Web site, and they were running ads for all of their charter advertisers. An interesting side effect was that the introduction of the Web site also solved the payment problem. Most of their customers now pay on time—it's one of the requirements for being considered a charter customer. Why? Because they don't get sales from the Web site unless they remain on that site by keeping their bills current. As a result, the revenue of the radio station has gone up—and in a market that the owner had said was totally saturated. In the future, he also may offer print ads for his charter clients. He is a solutions provider and he even has designed a form of one-stop marketing and sales solutions for all of his people.

ANOTHER CHICKEN SAGA

Here's a third and final story I want to share. Frank Perdue was a chicken producer, but there were already dozens of those in the country. He had a common commodity and his question was, "How can we differentiate this from all the other chicken producers?"

He sold dead chickens, so he was smart enough to say, "What's more of a commoditized product on the market than a dead bird?"

Frank Perdue, however, didn't stop with that obvious limitation. "How do I create a desire for the brand image of Perdue?" he asked an advertising firm. "What can we do to make us special so that our product stands out?"

Until then, Frank had taken out ads on radio, TV, and print, and said in effect, "At Perdue our chickens are plumper." (That's not necessarily true because they're getting the fowl from the same producers. The government calls that "puffery" and says it is all right to make such statements about your products.) There was nothing else he knew to say about his product.

He had to find a way to take his chickens from a pure commodity to continuous solutions development. He learned only one fact that made Perdue chickens different from any others on the market. He did not quick-freeze them and all of his competitors did.

"What happens when you quick-freeze chickens?" Frank was asked. "Why don't you freeze them as well?"

He shrugged. "Nothing's different. I don't like the quick-freeze process because it turns the bones black."

"Does the quick-freeze process impact the quality of the product?" they asked.

"Not one bit."

"How about the flavor? Does it change the flavor in any way?"

"Absolutely not. It has no impact whatever in quality or taste," he answered truthfully.

"So the only difference is that the quick-freeze chickens have black bones and your chickens don't." Perdue's ad people realized they had come up with the answer.

Soon, Frank Perdue appeared in his ads telling his housewife customers to look at the bones of the chicken they serve their family. If they were black, they weren't Perdue. Who wanted to serve their family a black-boned chicken? This didn't mean the Perdue chickens were better, tastier, or fatter, only that they were not quick frozen. The effect on the market was immediate.

Perdue was able to sell a commodity—a dead chicken—at a premium price, not because they sold a solution, but because they sold a solution to a problem they had created. This might mark the all-time best example of finding out what the problem is and solving it. Housewives don't want to serve blackboned chickens and are willing to pay a premium to the company who could fix it for them.

The other brands, such as Holly Farms and Tyson, caught up and stopped quick-freezing their chickens. Now what happens? The competition is equal again, although Perdue now has a recognized name.

This is where continuous solutions development functions. Perdue's company took the next step. They no longer offered just whole chickens, they created a new product—chicken parts. For instance, customers could buy only breasts. To make it easier, the company removed the bone and the skin, so cooking was easier and quicker. By doing this, they had created an almost-ready entrée for a meal.

Again, the others caught up. What did Perdue do next? They went from an "almost-ready entrée" to cooking those chicken parts. Now they offer harried families a cooked entrée. A mother rushing home from work only needed to add rice or noodles. After that, Perdue moved on to totally cooked whole meals.

As obvious as this may seem, let's look at what Frank Perdue did. He began with a commodity and continued to seek to turn it into a product. Once they had an identifiable product, they kept looking for new solutions to stay ahead of consumer demands.

From selling dead, non-frozen chickens at a commodity price, they kept asking, "What does the customer want? What are their needs?"

They realized that overscheduled people were saying, "Our lives are so fast-paced that we don't have time to start with a whole chicken and cook a delicious, nutritious meal anymore."

Perdue has provided a quality solution, and customers pay a premium for such solutions.

Frank Perdue and his company have caught the vision and they constantly redevelop themselves to provide solutions based on their customers' needs.

CREATE, INNOVATE, AND EXPAND

What has been the point of this chapter? Simply: Smart companies innovate. They continue to expand their customer base by solving problems for their customers.

When companies look at customers' needs instead of only at their own profit-and-loss statement, they provide solutions. The price of their product then goes up—often at a fairly rapid rate. This is called the generic model. The profit margin, or difference between costs and sales, increases even quicker, and that gap is called profitability. That is, the profitability is a lot higher the faster we get the solution.

For example, the profitability on the *second* Microsoft Office Software was more than 90 percent. The first one they put out, Windows, was very expensive. The second, Windows 95, was relatively inexpensive because it was a solution, not a commodity. The market forced the price down. Originally, their Windows software was expensive, but within months Windows appeared on almost every computer built. When that happened, Windows then became a commodity—until they brought out Windows 95, which was followed by Windows 98 and Windows ME, and they'll keep on developing.

Bear this also in mind. What makes a company beyond world class? It's not just solving problems. Beyond-world-class companies don't have problems that they must solve, because they solve them before they become problems.

PROBLEM SOLVERS, GOAL SETTERS, AND OPPORTUNISTS

To conclude this chapter, I want to point out three areas in the idea of continuous improvement, and I'll do it with questions.

1. How Do We Determine High-Order Solutions—The Kind That Move Us beyond the Commodity Stage?

Every company has the potential to move beyond the commodity stage. It's not always an easy task, and it takes a constant searching for answers and ways to solve problems for the customers we serve.

2. How Do We Develop an Internal Competence to Be Able to Look for High-Order Solutions?

By nature, people lean toward one of three methods when it comes to developing solutions. All three are valid approaches to developing high-order solutions, and we need all three.

The first question means they approach high-order solutions with one purpose. They are there to solve problems. Leadership consultant and author Bobb Biehl estimates that 80 to 85 percent of people lean to the problem-solving approach.

The second involves goal setting. Some people are more comfortable with setting goals to achieve high-order solutions. This concept focuses their attention on the prize and not the problem. Biehl estimates 10 to 15 percent of us have this tendency.

Finally, there are "opportunists." They tend to see the world in a completely different way than do the problem solvers and goal setters. Most often, opportunists are the ones who develop the highest order, out-of-the-box solutions. We usually call them the creative individuals, because they synthesize information, intuitively analyze it, and then "see" the solution.

If we increase our ability to analyze and solve problems, we can also learn to expand our ability to discover high-order solutions. Setting goals and then developing a plan to achieve those goals brings about high-order solutions. But the most effective process is to develop the talent of the opportunists. Every company has them. They are in almost every department and in every discipline.

The most important aspect of honing our skills is that we learn to develop high-order solutions. We learn to place ourselves outside the problem and to look inward. When we look for solutions from the right perspective, we often grasp the solution more clearly.

How do we do that thinking from outside the box? We do that when we're able to think like our customers' customers. This enables us to have a better view of what we have to do or what we can offer as a high-order solution.

When we combine these principles—the proclivity to problem solving, goal setting, and opportunism, along with the ability to use an inside-out perspective—we're amazed at the latent talent we find in our own organization.

3. How Do We Develop a Virtual Team Competence to Develop Those Solutions?

We form a virtual team when we combine people who are internal (inside the company) with those who are external (outside the organization), and their purpose is to develop a specific set of high-order solutions.

Some of the greatest, most profitable solutions have come about when we asked suppliers, potential suppliers, and employees to come together as a virtual team to solve a problem, develop a plan for achieving goals, and enable us to "see" a new opportunity.

Our suppliers, and often our customers, are usually delighted when we ask them to become part of a virtual team. Not only is it a sign of trust and loyalty, it sends the signal that we value their perspective and their input. Virtual teams are developed for a specific task, such as an ad hoc committee, so that once they have accomplished their purpose, the team is automatically broken up. That is, the team needs to be flexible, focused, and temporary so that they come together for a specific purpose and a defined result.

That is covenantal. That is maximizing the potential of the people in our organization. It also maximizes the potential on behalf of our customers, because we are then able to serve them at a higher level. When that happens, we become much more important to them.

One of the best and most cost-effective sources of solutions is a company's own supplier base. Although not part of the company, they can serve on virtual teams to maximize solutions development. Smaller companies are able to leverage their virtual team to create high-order and highly profitable solutions to their customers. Size is not as important as knowledge, creativity, and flexibility, which are all core components of the virtual team.

CHAPTER NINE

COVENANTING WITH EMPLOYEES

Does it really matter whether employees are satisfied with their jobs? It's amazing that many otherwise smart business leaders don't consider this a significant question. They emphasize satisfying the needs of their customers that results in more sales and higher profitability. If they satisfy their customers, what else matters?

When leaders worship at the altar of profitability, eventually they lose what they worship, because they have sacrificed the well-being of the very people who could increase their long-term profitability. Too many business leaders pay too little attention to correlating the power of good employee retention with the ongoing financial success of an organization. If they want to achieve long-term financial success, employee satisfaction isn't just good public relations—it's a primary ingredient.

Organizational leaders need to accept and promote the necessity of focusing on employees as well as customers. They need only to find out what makes any company a "best place to work."

When *Forbes* magazine presents its annual survey of the "100 Best Places to Work," the criteria they use to determine the winners reflect a bias toward sheer size. How can the vast majority of smaller, entrepreneurial, or emerging companies compete with some of the benefits that *Forbes'* chosen companies provide?

We know the answer. We know because we asked the most significant people involved in the question. That is, we asked employees and did in-depth interviews. We started with a simple question: "Tell us what matters most to you in your work."

This may surprise many, but they told us that what matters most wasn't the expensive benefits that larger companies can provide.

After surveying hundreds of employees in organizations as vastly different as heavy metal welding, fabrication companies, and insurance brokerage firms, we discovered six common factors that indicate employee satisfaction. We refer to three of them as foundational factors and the others motivational factors.

FOUNDATIONAL FACTORS THAT SATISFY

The big surprise was the first three factors we discovered, which we call *foundational factors*. When foundational factors are present, they seem to have little effect on morale or satisfaction. But when they're absent or, even worse, when they are taken away, morale and satisfaction drop significantly. These three foundational factors are:

1. Being paid well

2. Receiving good benefits, especially health benefits

3. Being assured of job security

Employees *expect* these benefits when they work for a company. That means that the rate of satisfaction doesn't increase significantly as those factors improve. However, when companies take away or decrease any of these three, that action seriously impacts—and sometimes permanently damages—employee satisfaction.

This means companies need to be careful about adding benefits and pay when times are good. If they can't sustain those benefits and must decrease the foundational factors, such action lowers satisfaction below the level it was prior to their addition. Too often, reductions in these factors tend to come about at times when the company is threatened, so the security factor exacerbates an already bad situation.

During the late 1980s, I was heavily involved in the turn-around market. Companies were right-sizing, downsizing, resizing, and in general butchering their people. One of the gravest mistakes most of the professional firms who helped with the cut-backs made was to decrease worker compensation after they downsized the firm. Not only were they asking people to do the work of two or even three people, but they increased their employees' insecurity by reducing their pay. Performance almost always dropped so that another round of cuts had to take place. Many formerly successful companies did not survive.

MOTIVATING FACTORS THAT SATISFY

We also discovered three *motivating factors* that are the most important indicators of long-term career satisfaction. Although not difficult to create, they take a concerted effort by the entire company leadership to make them a lasting reality. In fact, these factors are the employee foundation of a beyond-world-class company. Here are the motivating factors, which we will go into greater detail on.

1. Having Meaningful Work

Employees want to know that they're contributing something worthwhile to the organization. That is, they need to know that their work matters. In some jobs, it is easy to draw the connection to meaningful work. If the job is to save or protect lives, solve global problems, or invest in the education of future leaders, there is seldom a problem. But what about the millions of people who do the mundane, routine, and unglamorous jobs? What about those who keep a market economy humming? How can they draw meaning from their work?

The answer? It takes visionary leadership. By visionary leadership I don't mean the large, staring-off-into-the-distance type of vision. I am referring to what I call the living-the-vision variety.

Here's an old story, but it illustrates my point. It begins with three men digging ditches. The first is asked, "What is your job?"

He replies, "I am digging a ditch," and returns to his work.

The second replies, "I am digging a ditch that will join up with that man's ditch to make a larger ditch. We are working together." While a little more meaningful, it would be hard to see too much meaning in the work of the two ditch diggers.

The third man replies, "I am digging a ditch that will join with the ditches of two others and with many other ditches farther down the hill. Do you see that valley over there? When we are through, our ditch will carry the pipes that carry the water to quench the needs of a new city that is to be built down there."

All three do the same work, but the motivating factor is in place when they realize their work is meaningful, as well as recognize their contribution to the big picture.

This factor requires leaders to share the concept of the big picture with their employees. All work has mundane aspects, but it becomes meaningful when people recognize that they are part of a larger, more meaningful effort.

2. Being Part of a Community

Being part of a community is becoming increasingly important to more employees. This idea of community means they
want to enjoy the company of the people they work with—they
want to feel they belong. That perception of connectedness adds
a feeling of value to their lives. When we realize that most employees spend more time at their work places than they do so-
cializing within their own geographic communities, this idea
seems obvious.

There is power in community. Pastors tell us they would
like to create a sense of community within their churches. Social
workers remind us that what holds a family together is that the
kids thrive in an atmosphere of belonging. More than ever, people feel the need for connectedness. Companies can become the
communities we lost from simpler times. In fact, some already
have.

How can we make sure that the work gets done and yet foster a strong sense of community?

At Corporate Development Institute (CDI), we asked that
same question. We developed a program called Employee Satisfaction Surveys. Our results showed that organizations that foster a high level of community within the company consistently
outperform those that don't. It's just that simple. When employees feel they have a role within the work community, they show
increased morale, greater job satisfaction, and higher levels of
performance.

We can help to develop community by creating a conducive atmosphere. Even simple things such as coffee breaks and
holiday lunches can be powerful motivators. When individuals
feel that they're part of something—and such activities foster
that attitude—they respond positively.

We can *allow* community, or we can help to *create* it. When
we actively promote community, everyone wins and those benefits bring far greater returns than the investment of time and
money. When the employees of one client company got together

to raise money and build a Habitat for Humanity house, they created value and meaning far beyond what the owners would have ever imagined. They created community.

3. Providing an Opportunity for Career Advancement

People feel more satisfied if they know they have opportunities for growth in their career. Dead-end careers create dissatisfied employees. Companies need to provide opportunity for advancement and to commit themselves to sponsor employee development. That is, they need to take an active role in paving the road for employee promotion and growth. Too often career development is relegated to a human resources function when the power of it is a leverage tool that most leaders could use advantageously for increased performance.

One of the best methods for developing advanced career paths is to develop a system, such as the one we call Personal Development Plans. This forces the employees to be responsible for their own career development. Managers become sponsors by coaching and providing resources for career growth. Not only does it make better use of a leader's time, it creates a deeper sense of career responsibility within the employee.

Together these six foundational and motivational factors can determine whether a company will be a long-term success. Once leaders decide to make their company a "Best Place to Work" organization, they also need to evaluate their success on the measured satisfaction of employees.

Wise executives and managers know they can't ignore the correlation between long-term financial success and employee satisfaction. In fact, this correlation may be the most important resource a company can develop as it seeks to thrive in today's competitive marketplace.

Finally, think of the benefit of these six factors: Satisfied employees with high morale can withstand business downturns. They are the ones who can turn an average performance company into one that is high performance. What did our most loyal and best customers tell us was an indicator of good companies? Good employees with a high degree of morale and performance. Satisfied employees complete the success cycle. They are the real indicators for the long-term financial health and success of any organization.

Are you a "Best Place to Work" company? Maybe your employees know the answer.

COVENANTS WITH SUPPLIERS

If we consider employees as internal suppliers, we have already seen how a culture of covenant relations will develop a powerful service philosophy throughout the company. If we apply the same principles to our external suppliers, we increase the impact of that culture.

Most companies hold suppliers at arms' length, as if we're pushed back by our customers' buyers. (See Chapter 5, "Seeing the Customer's Future: Four Power Questions.") When we enter into a covenant with suppliers, an amazing thing happens. They look out for our best interest and seek ways to better serve us.

The principle of covenant is a principle that works in any relationship. When suppliers feel as though they're part of something and valued for more than offering the cheapest price, they increase their commitment to our success. The more people align with our vision and mission and the more people that help us, the more likely we are to succeed.

Here's an experience that illustrates this principle in a personal way. For several years I ran a furniture company I bought into as a turnaround opportunity. Once I had put my money on the table and left my successful job to become an entrepreneur, I learned that the situation was much worse than I had anticipated. The company had significant cash-flow problems and competency issues. To make matters worse, the economy was tanking.

In the midst of this, we muddled through. After months of juggling with cash issues, I finally felt that we might make it through the recession. I also realized I wasn't being covenantal with my suppliers. For instance, most terms we were given were Net 30. Because our terms to our customers were also Net 30, when they were slow paying, we were slow paying.

I decided that I had no right to assume that because my customers paid us slowly, that I could do the same. I wrote a letter to all of our suppliers, explained our current situation, and asked them to allow us to pay in 60 days until we could get caught up. Almost everyone agreed. Most of them wrote back and thanked me for communicating where we were and telling them how we anticipated getting back to terms.

One response blew me away. Mr. White was the owner of the company who supplied our finishes. Several weeks after he received my letter, Mr. White visited us with his salesman, whom we considered to be a partner, sharing his knowledge with our staff and helping us become the best in our industry at finishing.

After they arrived, we toured the plant. We shared our vision and our passion and thanked him for his support.

At the end of his visit, Mr. White shook my hand and said, "I want you to know how much I appreciated your letter. That's one of the reasons I wanted to come by and visit."

Here is the power of the covenant; he then asked, "Would it help you out if I gave you Net 90 terms for the next six months?"

The difference between Net 30 and Net 90 at our level of purchases meant he was offering us about a $75,000 interest-free loan, unsecured.

His words stunned me.

After I thanked him and saw them off, I realized that I had just experienced something we seldom hear of, let alone experience in the world of business today. I can tell you that even though I never visited his company, based on that visit and the actions of his salesman, Mr. White's company is beyond world class.

CHAPTER TEN

BUILDING A CHARACTER CULTURE

As organizations build a culture of character through covenantal relationships, they move toward becoming beyond world class.

Why do I keep stressing the importance of covenants? My use of the term means doing what's in the best interests of our suppliers, customers, and employees as they line up with our vision for our business ventures. By making covenants, this action becomes part of our continuous solutions. It's a matter of everyone winning because we're all working toward the same goals.

When this idea takes hold in our company, or any organization, and we pass this on to suppliers, customers, and employees, we have moved into the realm of building what I term the *character culture*. That is, we operate covenantly on every level. We respect ourselves and we respect the people we're involved with; in return, we receive their respect. Everyone wins if we set in place the covenantal culture.

Character culture refers to the environment created in a company because of the combined character of the people within that company. This also implies a greater emphasis on the character of the leadership.

Companies that create an open, caring, trusting, and flourishing environment do so because the leaders themselves are open, caring, and trustworthy, and they sponsor success in their people. They create environments conducive to learning, growth, and shared respect because such leaders are open to consider mistakes as opportunities for learning.

So how do we bring this about? How do we push beyond the merely theoretical and make it a practical reality?

Earlier, I pointed out that products and services change and adjust as the market fluctuates—they have to. I also stated the need to change policies based on customer needs—and they have to. One thing doesn't change, however—the principles by which we operate. Principles become our standards. The customers and the work change, and how we look at them changes, but I have to keep stressing that we remain firm on our values— our principles.

SIX PRINCIPLES OF CHARACTER CULTURE

At CDI, we've identified six guiding principles of character that are absolute essentials to this concept of covenantal relationships for employees. By using the term *employees,* I'm not excluding anyone. These are standards for every person connected with a company, beginning with the CEO and managers, and moving down to security guards and the mailroom. If everyone applies these principles, they can't help but affect the company's customers and suppliers.

At first these six guiding principles may seem simplistic and obvious. But if that is true, why don't we observe them more often in action? They're difficult to bring about, especially in a corporate climate where the impersonal easily obscures the need for the personal.

This is also a call to change—a call for everyone to embrace the six principles. In presenting them, we're the first to acknowledge that people resist change. That's why earlier I said it's hard to do. It *is* hard to do. Even knowing that, we're asking people to modify their behavior and to have their outlook transformed for their good and for the good of the organization.

I'll go into more detail in the remaining chapters, but the six goals that organizations need to keep in mind to bring about this much desired culture are:

1. *Humility.* We focus on the needs and situations of others—but at the same time don't think less of ourselves.

2. *Sponsoring champions.* Leaders set the example and that enables employees to follow. Those leaders seek out and support others within the organization that show potential. When they recognize outstanding ability, they "champion" the advancement of the best.

   In covenantal employee relations, our job isn't to guarantee employment. Our responsibility isn't to keep people employed forever. It's also not to give them the highest pay that we can and then not hold them accountable. Our responsibility is to do what is in the best interest of the employee based on the higher purpose of the company, and this includes a concern for their personal destiny.

3. *Integrity.* This concept goes far beyond being truthful. Integrity means complete top-to-bottom alignment between the goals and objectives of the company and the personal destiny of its employees.

   Many look at the word integrity and think it's a synonym for *honesty.* That's true, but let's take it a little deeper. When it comes to business, for me, the word means integrated—together, unified, and all in one. Too many of our companies are dis-integrated with confusing policies and a variety of products they're not sure will fit. Then they try to build business principles around those situations. I think they're looking at this backward.

4. *Modeling.* Employees, customers, and suppliers must see covenantal behavior modeled throughout the company before such qualities can permeate the company. Leaders are the models. When they balance these principles while producing outstanding results, the culture is transformed.

5. *Fairness.* Closely aligned with caring is the principle of fairness. People who are treated fairly are more likely to support the decisions and requirements of leaders who ask them to step outside their comfort zone.

6. *Caring.* This old-fashioned concept is a powerful tool for employee encouragement and growth.

CHAPTER ELEVEN

CHARACTER CULTURE
Humility

If an organization had to choose one principle that would most immediately impact the entire character of the company, I'd say it should be humility. This is also the most difficult to incorporate in a me-generation society.

Part of the problem is that we don't teach humility anymore in this country. What we teach in business school is pride. It's win, win, and win again. In fact, the message of win-win is even stronger: For us to win, our competitors must lose. It's victory for us in order to succeed and there is no place for anything less than defeating our competition.

Is it surprising then, that I say we've become a society that doesn't understand humility?

"What is humility?" Ever ask that question? If we did— whether to employees or coworkers—we might be amazed at the responses. What they define as humility translates into weakness or the inability to stand up for what we believe. It's being the person who never makes waves or creates problems and let's everyone else make the decisions.

That's not my concept of humility.

HUMILITY—A FOCUSED STRENGTH

Here's Corporate Development Institute's (CDI) definition: *Humility is thinking highly of the other person without thinking less of yourself.* It's not so much a matter of them first and me second or vice versa. It's really a matter of pressing toward both at the same time, and it happens. We don't have to sacrifice one for the other.

Once we understand who we are, we can assess ourselves more clearly. We can claim our earned successes, and that's not boasting, because it's accepting part of who we are. Humility is knowing our strengths and focusing them for the good of others. Too often humility has become synonymous with weakness when, in fact, it is anything but weak.

Humility also means that our understanding and concern don't stop with our success, our goals, and our need to achieve. Part of our success is respect and concern for the same needs and achievements in other people. If we can take others' situations into account—and understand them and seek the best for them—that's humility.

Maybe I don't need to spend so much time on this working definition, but it's difficult for many to grasp because they unconsciously think of themselves as selfish if they want to achieve success. Consequently, they miss the point. Humility is first acknowledging who we are and what we can do, and then moves on to acknowledging those qualities in others. Humility isn't denying our abilities or hiding our talents.

If I am a great salesperson, for instance, humility doesn't say, "I'm not a very good salesperson, just a lucky one." Instead, I get great satisfaction when I am in my element, working with customers, and using my strengths to bring success to my company.

Humility is not thinking less of ourselves, but it's understanding ourselves and leveraging our strengths. It's also not thinking less of the other person. It's certainly not the old idea we hear of putting others first—which is impossible anyway—

but it does imply a commitment to understand, nurture, and build up their strengths as we enhance our own.

Humility isn't denigrating our God-given skills and talents, but it accepts them and then goes a step farther—we seek the talents in others.

I've put these two concepts together—humility and seeking the highest potential in others—because they are the foundation for living and working in covenantal relationships. We must have both.

When I see both of these attributes, I no longer have to focus all my energies on myself or on promoting myself. In seeking to make all of us successful, I am moving toward true humility.

Isn't it sad that humility isn't something we teach in business school? It's not something we teach in company training programs. It's not even something that we've been teaching in our churches. Yet it is at the base of covenantal relationships.

At CDI, we realized that if we asked, "What is humility?" our question would push people to think in the wrong direction. So we devised questionnaires to indicate the humility factor. Instead of asking, "Is your boss humble?" we asked, "In most situations, does your boss consider the needs of others?"

We have follow-up queries to make sure they understand what we want to know. Over the years, we've developed surveys that can fairly well show that humility factor.

I want to take this concept of humility to a practical level. Humility doesn't self-promote, but it comes in and says, "I'm going to look out for the best interests of others on behalf of our organization. I'm part of that organization. If this is good for the organization, then it's good for me."

Here's an example of what I mean. I met a man I'm going to call Mitch, and he's a good speaker—in fact, he's an excellent oral communicator—and besides, he's someone who has significant things to say.

In the years he's worked for his company, he has never promoted himself as an oral communicator because he wanted to be humble. He had what I regard as a sense of false humility. What he didn't grasp is that if this ability was good for the organization, he was responsible to make his talent known. That way, he could have done the best for himself and the company at the same time by saying, "I think I can communicate well before an audience." Instead, he waited for someone to see this ability and promote him.

That promotion never happened.

When I met with Mitch, I sensed a lot of bitterness because no one within the organization had recognized his ability, or if they did, no one pushed him to use it.

"The trouble is that you're confusing your sense of humility with the fact that you're the one who's supposed to put forward your best on behalf of the organization," I explained. "Why didn't you make it known to people that you had that ability?"

"I didn't want people thinking I was, you know, proud and all that."

After a lengthy interview, I said to Mitch, "Here's what we're going to do. I know you're a little bitter, and you need to accept that most of that is your responsibility for not opening up. But we're going to help you. We're going to feature you as a keynote speaker at the next organization conference."

"But—but, no, no, no. I mean, I can't . . ."

"Yes, you can. This is what you've been waiting for, isn't it?"

He nodded and then started to protest again.

"Listen, Mitch. We're going to give you the opportunity to show your ability. You're going to stop whining and complaining. Instead, focus on having something positive to say. You can do that because you do have something to say. Be bold about it."

The last time I spoke with Mitch he was preparing for a conference where he would speak before 600 business leaders. He was terrified.

I was delighted.

He has something to say and now he's learning that humility is to admit, "I can do this."

CHAPTER TWELVE

CHARACTER CULTURE
Sponsoring Champions

Once humility becomes part of the culture, the principle of sponsoring champions becomes the method of moving this concept throughout the entire company.

For me, the term means that we constantly encourage others who have abilities. We intentionally work with them for their advancement within the company.

I love to see an organization where people who do similar jobs spot those who have special ability, get behind them, and help them get ahead. They're the ones who go to their supervisors or managers and thus "sponsor" the champions they see.

SPONSORS BEGET SPONSORS

My cowriter for this book, Cecil ("Cec") Murphey, caught on to this idea while we were working together. He has been a ghostwriter for about 15 years. Individuals like me or publishers come to him to use his talents to help others write their material.

In the past, he has had two major struggles. When he began doing this full-time, he was financially insecure and said yes to almost every project. He admits that occasionally a project didn't work out well. As he moved along, he began to listen more carefully to each business proposition. After one particularly disastrous project, he realized that making a profit was only one consideration. Although he didn't use the term *covenantal*, in that extremely difficult situation, the person he worked with wasn't what he called "honorable."

Cec has since moved to the next step—that of sponsoring champions. When he is offered a book project, he does a serious self-study and asks, "Is this a viable project? If so, is it something I can do well? Or is there someone who can do it better than I can?" Ghostwriting is a highly specialized and extremely competitive field, but he had decided he would not make other ghostwriters his competitors.

In the spring of 2001, he was offered a lucrative project, and the more he researched the topic and the person, the more exciting it sounded. Everything indicated the man who approached him would form a covenantal relationship.

There was still one factor left for him to consider. As he asked, "Is there someone who can do a better job?" he knew the answer. Although he knew he could do an adequate job and satisfy the client, he knew another person who could write an even better book for that person.

"I love the idea and it's great," Cec told the client, "but I know a man named Jim who can do this better than I can." He told the client how to get in contact with Jim and added, "If he says no, will you contact me? I'd like to do the book if he turns you down."

Jim took the project.

A week later, a woman came to Cec with a five-book offer. Again, it was a situation where he knew he could do it, but he also knew a woman named Sue who, in his opinion, would be able to take the books from "good" to "excellent." Sue is doing the five-book project.

Cec also points out that he has not lost business by using this process. The day after he suggested Sue, an outstanding project came his way that he would otherwise have had to turn down because of time commitments.

This story focuses on the concept of sponsoring champions, even those we could call our competitors. When we see someone who has great potential, we need to sponsor them.

In corporate America, we also need to protect them so that when they stumble and struggle, we can lift them up and encourage them to keep trying. This means that we seek to sponsor those around us so that we can help them maximize *their* success. We live in such a competitive world that many have laughed at such a concept.

This is the heart of being covenantal. It's being able to say to someone, "You have a great career ahead of you. I recognize your ability and I'm going to sponsor you."

When individuals within an organization sponsor champions, the company also takes a giant step forward. It means that the company can be more successful than their competitors. It gives employees better incentives to work hard and to remain loyal, because they know their mentors look out for their interests.

This sponsoring of others also avoids the stress of trying to show ourselves better than others, or needing to beat the competition within the organization, or striving to outrun the outside competition.

We've lost that sponsoring champions concept in organizations because we've bought into the idea of "What's in it for me?" Or we say, "No one ever did that for me, so why should I do it for anyone else?"

The laws of God (or if you prefer, call them laws of the universe) operate with a strange kind of justice. Those who give the most to others are the ones who get the most in return.

Too many live in a frenzied state of fear because they believe they have to compete for a limited prize. And we're not limited! It's not a matter of there being only one customer or one contract out there. We're competing for unlimited prizes, and therefore we can—and ought to—sponsor talented individuals.

People who excel in leadership recognize talents in others. They can resent and fear them or they can put those able people in leadership. Such leaders win because they bring out the best in others.

A BOOST UP THE LADDER OF SUCCESS

Hal (not his real name) was the boss I liked the least of any I worked for in the first 20 years of my business life. He became my boss after he hired me as vice president of marketing in a large furniture manufacturing company. Part of my responsibility was to oversee and sell the well-known brands that came from one plant and were shipped all over the globe.

Hal was sometimes verbally abusive and compulsive. Even worse, he was dangerous, because we never knew how to expect him to react to situations. Despite those negative qualities, that man also taught me what it meant to sponsor champions.

After I had been with the company a few weeks, he called me into his office. "Son, I'm going to give you many opportunities to succeed. I don't know your limits, and this is your chance to learn those limits for yourself. There is just one thing: I want you to come back and tell me when you're in water that's over your head. You tell me when you've screwed up and don't try to hide that from me. If you'll share that information with me, I'll back you all the way. But you still are responsible for your own success."

"Why, thank you . . ." I started to reply.

"Don't ever lie to me!"

"No, sir, I . . ."

". . . and if you ever misuse any of the company's resources, or you ever get complacent, I'll fire you."

I nodded, still excited about his confidence in me.

"I'll be watching you. You've got a chance, so make the most of it," he offered as he dismissed me from his office.

Hal meant every word he spoke. What he didn't say was that although he gave me the opportunity to succeed (and I wasn't the only recipient of his help), he vigilantly watched every one of us and waited for us to fail. If we made one mistake and didn't tell him, we were out. He had warned me that he would be watching, but I hadn't expected quite such vigilance. Hal offered no second chances.

Another thing I didn't like about Hal was that he created competition between the top performers. As we got better at our jobs, he put us in the arena with each other and said, in effect, "You two fight it out. One of you will win."

Hal loved seeing the competition and enjoyed watching to see who would win and who would lose.

Yes, I learned from him. Not only did I learn about negative leadership, but the positive thing I learned was what I later began to call sponsoring champions.

Hal sponsored me. I'm not sure what he saw in me, but he made it clear that he picked me for my ability and wanted me to have the chance to make the most of myself. He gave me the opportunities, and both of us knew that the rest of it was up to me.

I kept my part of the covenant, even though I hadn't yet begun to use that word. I never lied to him. A couple of times I had to say, "Hal, I'm in over my head."

He accepted that statement and took off some of the pressure. With almost the next breath, he would challenge me to grow.

Despite all the negative things I could say about my feelings for Hal, he gave me enormous opportunities and, consequently, I became successful.

What a number of other employees in that company didn't know was that I made mistakes—and a couple of them were what I'd call "seriously big." But no one ever knew about them. My boss covered for me. He never told anyone or used those failures against me because I kept my promise to him. As soon as I knew when I'd messed up, I'd rush to his office and say, "Man, did I screw up."

Hal would listen to my story and his next question was, "How much did it cost me?"

"About a million bucks," I said the first time, "and nearly $4 million of revenue." In reality, the costs were much higher, because the failure kept a very promising program from being launched.

"That's a pretty high learning cost, Alan. Now what did you learn from this?"

After I told him, he'd nod and ask, "Okay, what are you going to do about it?" He didn't mean that I should try to fix the problem—it was too late for that. He wanted to know what I would do so that it would never happen again.

This final question forced me to do some serious soul searching. He wouldn't have tolerated any shallow response. Finally, I'd figure out ways to avoid such costly mistakes again. Then he'd send me back to try again.

For me, it was painful and humiliating to admit I had failed. Sometimes his language became abusive, but he had kept his word and always backed me.

In a strange way, Hal's faithfulness in backing me helped me grasp the idea of sponsoring champions, because it dawned on me what he had given me—despite the negative factors. I thought, I can do that for people too.

In his bid to sponsor champions, Hal failed to grasp that because of a fear of failure, many potential champions never take risks.

One peer, whom I'll call Ron, made a less serious mistake, and it had far less impact than my bad decision. Out of fear, however, he hid the mistake from Hal. Once it became evident, Ron tried to blame others. He was so afraid of the ramifications of his failure that he destroyed his credibility, his integrity, and his potential. After 17 years as a successful regional vice president, Hal eventually forced Ron out of the company.

SPONSORING CHAMPIONS AND COMPANY ALIGNMENT

As I've moved ahead in my life, sponsoring champions has been part of a centerpiece of the covenant idea.

Here's how I do it. When I spot a champion, I ask, "What is it that you want? Where do you want to go in the company?"

Sometimes employees don't know the answer. In fact, I'm shocked at how few of them do. Part of sponsoring them may mean we have to connect them with their purpose. If their personal purpose is to make a million dollars in the next three years, it won't fit with our intrinsic purpose. They'll abuse customers and other people.

If their idea is, "I want a secure place where I can work and be valued as an employee long term," they probably will fit.

Let's say a woman is working in our accounting department and I ask, "What is it that you want?"

"I want to be a country and western singer," she replies.

That person may be extremely talented in music, and perhaps just as talented in the accounting department, but if her goal is to become a singer, she won't fit with our long-term vision.

It's amazing how little attention is paid to this matter when companies offer jobs. It's also amazing what can happen in companies when there is a good fit of employee and company.

In the short run, the would-be singer could line up with our goals. But how could we most benefit that person? We could probably help her more if we guided her toward her quest to become a singer. But she'll never fit long term with us, because we're not a company that needs singers.

Consequently, there's a lot of disconnection between the purpose of the organization, now defined by the goals and objectives, and the personal destiny of the employees. What we have to do as leaders is to balance those factors—and in so doing, we need to keep in mind these three questions:

1. What is in the best interest of the company?

2. What is in the best interest of the employee?

3. How can we make the most of combining the answers to the first two questions?

Perhaps the following story will illustrate this. For obvious reasons, I've changed the identity of the person.

In the mid-1990s, I was president of an organization called Fellowship of Companies for Christ International (FCCI). We had started as a small organization that brought in several hundred thousand dollars a year and grew at such a rapid pace until millions of dollars poured through our accounts.

Edward had come on board as a bookkeeper when we were still a small company. Over the next few months, everything changed, including our financial system. It seemed as if overnight we went from small to big, from simple to complicated. Not only did the financial and accounting control system change, the need for people to manage those accounts changed. We needed an accountant—in fact, we were really behind by not hiring one.

I sat down with Edward, who expressed great frustration over the changes. He made a point that he was doing the same kind of work that he had done when we hired him and that we had known his capabilities when we hired him. Now, he complained, we were trying to force him to become something else.

"This just isn't fair to me. I've been a loyal employee, and I've always done everything you've asked. Sometimes, I've even stayed late and not asked for overtime pay."

I agreed and listened to his litany of complaints.

"What you're not acknowledging is that the needs of FCCI have changed," I said. "Our goals and objectives have grown and you can't stop that change. That's why we're in business, and it's a good thing. Wouldn't you agree that where we are and where we're going is a good thing?"

"Well, yes, of course," he agreed.

"And because you're an employee of FCCI, I want you to be part of our growth."

"Okay," he said.

"But for that to happen, you have to change. I would like for you to upgrade your bookkeeping skills."

We had an education assistance program that paid for people to earn their GED, go to college, or get training to help them advance.

He started telling me how busy he was already with family obligations and the classes he was taking at college.

"It's like this, Edward. We need you to upgrade your skills to go from being a bookkeeper to an accountant. You're still able to do the work we need done, but you won't be able to keep up much longer. Furthermore, we're going to need a comptroller and eventually a CFO. I'm not sure that you'll ever make CFO, and I'm not sure that you'll ever make the role of comptroller. But I do think you can go from being a bookkeeper to an accountant. For that to happen, you need technical skills and a lot more knowledge about accounting. You're an excellent bookkeeper and when we were small, you were exactly what FCCI needed.

Our needs have changed and that means you have to change to move along with us."

We talked quite a bit and I also told him that I needed a person with accounting skills to fulfill the purpose of our company. "You can be that person, and I think it's in your best interest if you go back to business school."

For several minutes we sat in silence, until Edward said, "I'd like to be the accountant." He then told me that he was already going nights to college to earn a degree. "You see, the problem is that the courses I'm taking are in health administration. I'm less than a year from having my degree."

"You need to make a decision," I said.

Edward never came back to see me, but the office manager did. She said, "Edward has decided he wants to continue taking health administration courses and working for his degree in that area."

I needed someone immediately with accounting skills and I couldn't put this off. I asked Edward to come to my office. "I've got two choices. I'm going to hire an accountant to replace you, or I can wait patiently until you develop the needed skills. I estimate that would take you anywhere from six months to a year. What I can't do is allow the company to pay for you to continue to take health administration courses and deny that we need accounting skills now."

Edward was good at what he did, but being good at the old job wasn't enough.

"What is your dream job, Edward? If you could have any job you want, what would it be?"

His eyes lit up. "That's easy. I want to be an administrator in a health organization." He launched into a full minute of spontaneous excitement about his dream.

When he stopped, I said, "Okay, this is what I'm going to do. I'm going to hire your replacement. I'm asking that you stay on board until that person is trained. You're free to leave now, but I would ask that you stay on board because I don't know how long it's going to take. At least right now, you're doing the bookkeeping job. I trust you and value you as an employee, but the minute that I hire somebody, I'm going to give you a 60-day notice. I'll need you to stay for 30 of those days and help train that person in our system. The last 30 days you'll be paid and you can do whatever else you want to do."

Instead of Edward being happy about my offer, he became quite upset. "This isn't fair, you know," he said several times.

"When we hired you, we explained to you the nature of covenant. As an employee you covenanted with FCCI to provide the services that we needed in this organization. As the leader, I'm telling you the services I need are changing because the organization is changing. You cannot continue to hold your job if you function in the old manner. I need an accountant and I need a comptroller, and I need them as soon as possible. However, I understand your desire to go into health administration. If you stay while we hire and train your replacement—which could take six months—we will continue to pay for your education in health administration."

"All right," he said, but it was obvious that he still wasn't happy.

Edward stayed, and he was a covenantal employee. I trusted him and he continued to do his job well. We hired someone a little more than two months after our first talk, and then it took another two months to train the person, and we gave Edward an additional two months of work after that.

Finally, I went to Edward and said, "We cannot afford a bookkeeper and an accountant. I only need one person for this job."

He was angry and insisted it was an unfair termination.

Covenantally as the leader, I followed through and gave him everything that we had promised. He actually violated his covenant with us by his bitter attitude and by making it extremely difficult for his replacement to learn the job.

About a year later, Edward's former supervisor came to me and said, "Guess who I saw at the mall yesterday?" She had talked with Edward.

"Really. What's he doing?"

"He has a great job. He's the Assistant Administrator at Clayton Medical Center. And he pointed out that he's making 20 percent more money than he made here, even though he's still in a starting position, and he has great advancement opportunities."

"How's his attitude?"

"Wonderful. In fact, I've never known him to be this happy before. He loves what he's doing. He has his degree now and he's using the education he worked so hard for."

This true story illustrates how sometimes even employees don't know that what we're doing is in their best interest. If I had kept Edward as our bookkeeper, I wouldn't have serviced FCCI well, and he would have remained unhappy in his work. I'm not sure if he would ever have left if I hadn't forced him to.

Here's the other part—the sad part. Edward never came back to say, "Thank you for helping me to fulfill my destiny and to get the job I love." He never said, "Thanks for helping me stay true to my personal destiny."

Regardless, we helped Edward to align his personal destiny. Even though we had to do it outside of the company, we did the right thing for everyone concerned.

That's the definition of a covenantal relationship with an employee. Sometimes it's hard. Sometimes termination works in the best interests of everyone.

THE GUIDING PRINCIPLES OF SPONSORING CHAMPIONS

I want to detail four guiding principles we need to bear in mind when we sponsor champions.

1. Those We Sponsor Must Be Champions

We can't take mediocrity and make it super quality. We don't choose people because they have nice smiles or because they get along well with others at work. We choose them because they have that something called quality or talent or ability that makes them stand out in their job.

For instance, if I can run a mile in eight minutes and there is someone on the team who can run it in five, that person is the champion. I can run every day and get the best training, buy first-quality running shoes, and hire the world's top trainer. Despite all that help, I'm not likely to win the race. I'll probably never run a mile in five minutes, and so I could never beat that special runner in a race.

However, suppose my coach comes to me and says, "I know you're an eight-minute-a-mile runner, Alan. With a little extra effort, I think we can make you into a seven-minute-a-mile runner." That coach understands my capabilities as a champion.

In effect, the coach is saying, "You're not a champion in the five-minute race, but we can make you a champion on your level."

We need to recognize who to sponsor. We don't hinder the rise of average workers, but we sponsor outstanding individuals.

Not everybody is a champion, and despite hundreds of opportunities, some people will never prove themselves capable of top jobs. That's unfortunate, but it's true. That fact doesn't denigrate anyone—not everybody wants to be a champion.

I know of people who catch on to the championship idea and want to make champions out of everyone, but they fail in their efforts because they try to challenge people beyond their comfort level.

2. There Must Be an Opportunity for Them

If no openings exist, it's difficult to sponsor champions. We don't sponsor people to become comptrollers by saying, "Okay, count every coin that comes into our company. We want a list by pennies, nickels, and so on." We sponsor them by giving them chances to grow in the field where they have talent.

3. We Have to Be Able to Give Them Resources

If we believe someone has the ability, and we ensure that they have the opportunity, but we don't give them the resources, we have failed them, the company, and ourselves. Too many organizations give people the dangling-carrot opportunity and hold out a great future for them. However, by not providing adequate resources, we actually put obstacles in their path.

4. We Have to Expect and Anticipate Mistakes

I want to say this stronger: We need to *cherish* those mistakes made by our champions. We're giving them the supreme vote of confidence. When we uphold them in the low, discouraging times, that's when we function best as champion sponsors.

We can't sponsor champions by not allowing for mistakes. Like my old boss did with me, we need to allow for mistakes and help them figure out what they can learn from them. Hal was a champion sponsor.

A story that has circulated in the business world illustrates this nicely. As I've heard the story, it goes like this: Jack Welch, head of General Electric, championed for the creation of a new division. The new division was one of the "skunk works" described by Tom Peters, where resources are given to champions to take risks, think big, and develop new opportunities.

The story says that Jack Welch pulled a champion out of another division and put him at the head of the skunk works. After two years, and spending $26 million, the new division head still hadn't created the product Welch had anticipated.

GE pulled the plug.

The sponsored champion went into Welch's office. "I'm sorry. I know you trusted me and I told you that this would be a great division. I thought it would be. We ran into things we didn't understand, and I let you down." He held out a sheet of paper, "Here's my resignation."

Welch grabbed the paper and tore it up without reading it. "You've got to be crazy. We've just spent $26 million teaching you. And you think I'm going to let you go to a competitor?"

They reassigned that champion.

The story also has circulated that when Thomas Edison invented the light bulb, that wasn't the solution he was working toward. Before he came up with a light bulb, he recorded more than 1,600 mistakes.

Isn't that sometimes how we learn—by making mistakes?

Of course, if the mistakes are so costly they put the organization out of business, that's different. It is also the responsibility of the sponsor not to let the potential champion "bet the farm." We cannot let champions take risks with resources that will cripple the company.

SPONSORING PEERS

Here are two final thoughts on this matter. First, I want to emphasize that in covenantal companies, we need to search for others' maximum potential all the time—and that requires humility on our parts. When we sponsor champions, it says, "I'll select the few uniquely outstanding individuals, and I'll help them to be successful for the good of our company. In helping them, they may turn out to be my bosses. That's okay, because it will work best for all of us."

Second, perhaps I've implied this, but I want to point out that this principle works with sponsoring peers.

We have to recognize two components when we focus on sponsoring peers. The more powerful component is that we're willing to recognize the strengths in a coworker and do something about it. That means we go to our boss or supervisor and say, "You've got me doing this project, I'd like to do this and I'll do a good job, but I honestly believe that Kevin can handle this far better than I can. Could you put Kevin on my team? That way, if I'm wrong about his ability, I'll step in and fix it."

Here's another thing we can do to sponsor. We start by giving credit to others for their excellence. Suppose I go to my boss and say, "I want you to know about the excellent work Angela is doing." We do that even if the person is doing the same job as we are.

To do this requires me to put my selfish, vested interest behind me. It's hard to do that. In the corporate structure it looks as if we're all vying for the next higher slot together.

I have found that those who sponsor champions become the leaders of the future. There may be a few glitches before they get there, and they may have a few bosses that take advantage of them. In a beyond-world-class company, we recognize and we reward. As part of that, we also acknowledge the developers and mentors.

Here's the ultimate test for sponsoring peers for each of us.

Am I willing to go to a peer and say, "I think you have great potential in what you're doing. How can I serve you in reaching your maximum potential? How can I serve you in your best interests on behalf of something that will be good for you?" I may not gain from this, but I'm doing the right thing and the best thing. I'm acting as part of a mutual covenant.

When that happens, there's an extremely good chance that my peer will say to my boss, "You know what? Alan sponsors champions. He's challenged me and he's supported me. One of the reasons I've done so well in this job is because of Alan."

The risk we take in sponsoring is that it doesn't always have a happy ending. One day that champion may stand on the platform and take all the credit. That sometimes happens. But we will know the truth and we will also know that we did what we could. We may even have to remind ourselves that we didn't do it to get something in return. We sponsored because we believed it was the right thing for us to do.

We'd all like to have the credit we're due. We may or may not get it. Some of us who were sponsored may forget who gave us our chance. We can become bitter and complain, or we can take satisfaction in knowing we did the right thing and that we did what was best for the company.

Frankly, the ultimate test for champion sponsors is that we find great joy in the success of others and in maximizing their potential. We make it clear in the beginning that we're not doing this to get something from them. Most people are good enough to credit us for our help.

But not everyone does. Not everyone will. If they don't give us the credit, they have not violated anything. Even though they may not give us the recognition, we have something far more lasting—it's called intrinsic reward.

We will know we did the right thing.

That in itself can bring an immense amount of satisfaction.

CHAPTER THIRTEEN

CHARACTER CULTURE
Integrity and Modeling

Let's define integrity as the quality that enables us to keep the covenant regardless of the costs. That's easier to say than it is to demonstrate because we've dumbed down integrity in our society.

In practical terms, integrity says, "I won't lie to a customer." But I mean more than that. Integrity also means I will keep my end of the covenant regardless of the cost and regardless of the actions of others. I am willing to walk away from recognition as well as possible growth in my business. It's being able to say, as I had to say to a lot of people who were depending on Sklar Pepplar, "We cannot deliver this in September as promised."

I want to go back to the Sklar Pepplar incident (see Chapter 3). I didn't know that I was defining integrity for our organization. I didn't feel good about what I had to do, but I did it anyway. As I mentioned earlier, this happened when I was in the middle of my struggle over whether to deceive the VIP group or tell them the truth. If I had deceived the VIP buyers, I would have been a man of lying (or unclean) lips.

After I told the truth and faced the scorn of many, one man understood. He was a man of integrity and had recognized that I had done the right thing, no matter what I had cost Sklar Pepplar in lost revenue.

He said the magic words to me: "You know, lad, you did exactly what Lou Sklar would have done in the old days. The reason we stopped doing business with Sklar Pepplar is because they lost that great sense of doing the right thing. But don't you be worrying. We're going to do a lot of business with Sklar Pepplar. You're a company of integrity again."

I had done the right thing—and that's integrity—even though I had hesitated, wondered, and even feared about the outcome. Integrity *is* doing the right thing regardless of the outcome.

In that instance, Ian recognized us as a company of integrity. It's unfortunate, but that wasn't true—we weren't a company of integrity. I know how most of the employees would have responded—they would have lied or at least deceived. This isn't meant to speak against them. They would have done what they considered the prudent thing. For me, it was a test of my integrity.

That then leads me to point out that being a beyond-world-class company isn't just about one leader of integrity leading a company forward. Beyond-world-class companies are those in which integrity is endemic, systemic, and works completely throughout the organization. I think of it as blood coursing through the entire body. Where there is a lack of integrity, it's obvious to everyone.

GENERATIONAL INTEGRITY

Here is another illustration of integrity on the line. A man I'll call Jacob succeeded his father as the head of a company. He followed someone who was highly respected as a man of deep integrity.

When I agreed to work with Jacob—and I already had worked with his father many times before—I wondered if he understood the covenant values as deeply as his father had.

I soon learned.

Our company, Corporate Development Institute (CDI), came to help Jacob's company transition a merger within the financial services division. This merger naturally concerned everyone.

Additionally, Jacob's people didn't know where they were in the process, because they hadn't had any dealings with the people who wanted to merge with them. When we met with the management team to discuss all their concerns, we especially wanted to make sure we were covenantal in this venture.

A member of the management team said, "I want to bring a man here who knows these people. He'll tell us what they're really like."

I knew what he was doing. He was trying to set everyone against the people who wanted to merge. He went on and on, never quite calling them unethical or saying anything that would nail down anything wrong.

As I listened, I could hardly believe what I was hearing. For some time, I had known he was the weakest part of the team— that is, my research from suppliers and customers indicated that he was the weak link in management and that some of his ethics had been questionable.

My immediate reaction was to jump up and yell, "No! We won't let that happen. We don't bring somebody here to talk against others. We don't even know the man who wants to talk to us against them. What if he's bitter or carries a grudge?"

I didn't do that. I sat there, the anger rising. I could hardly believe that anyone would want to bring in someone to sneak behind the backs of the people who had approached the company in good faith—or had so far as I knew.

None of the other team members said anything. One of them nodded and another shrugged.

For the first time, Jacob spoke up. He had only recently become CEO and this was his first important meeting. "You're not bringing anyone in here to do that."

"Well, a couple of us talked about it. We just want to . . ."

"You're not bringing that man in here. This company does not stand for such tactics."

Everyone sat in stunned silence.

"Let me ask you something," Jacob said, and turned to face each of them one at a time. "If my father were in this seat, would you have tried to do this?"

Everybody looked down. No one said a word.

Within minutes the tone of the meeting changed. The calculating team member left the room to tell the "witness" he wouldn't be invited to speak. After he returned, so far as I'm aware, he didn't say another word in the meeting.

Another interesting thing happened. Each of the other members of the team turned to Jacob and said, in a variety of ways, "Please forgive me. I can't believe we would put you in that place or that we didn't see what was happening."

That's when it became obvious that several members of the team had conspired together to stop the merger and, I assume, had done so largely because of one man's influence. When they left the meeting, they had changed. Because of the leadership example, they understood integrity—they saw it demonstrated in front of them.

Since that meeting, Jacob has gotten phone calls from team members—all department heads. Typical is one leader who said to him, "That was an eye-opening meeting for me. I didn't realize that I had overstepped the bounds. By allowing it to happen, I lacked integrity. I wouldn't have realized that fact if you had kept silent."

Operating with integrity often throws us into tough situations. One of the things I've recognized right next to integrity is accountability. Each of us needs people around us who hold us accountable for our actions. Jacob did that for the team members, and he could do it only because of his own sense of integrity.

We live in a world where gray can look more like black or white. It's not a black-and-white world, and at times we have to make decisions and decide the right thing to do. That's when we act with integrity.

I need people to hold me accountable to make the right decisions. I need to be accountable to them, and when that happens, they will support me no matter what the cost.

FREEDOM TO FAIL

Before we move on from the matter of integrity, I want to focus on mistakes. It is important to understand the difference between a willful lack of integrity and the fact that someone has simply made a mistake.

Once we understand the difference, we will not allow willful mistakes to take place because of disregard for integrity and values, thus violating our covenant with employees, suppliers, or customers.

For instance, if I see a mistake, I need to determine if it was done while pursuing the right objectives. If I'm convinced the person was intentionally violating the covenant, I cannot tolerate it. I may need to terminate that person.

But what about honest mistakes? Jim Webb, a former employee of Procter and Gamble, relayed a story to me that best illustrates this idea. Whenever anyone at Procter and Gamble made a serious mistake—a mistake made with integrity—the company didn't ignore it. Instead, throughout the company's loud speaker system, everyone heard the recording of a cannon being fired. They celebrated because they believed someone had learned something and, consequently, they all had learned something.

If I give people the freedom to make mistakes, but at the same time, I put them at risk for doing it, then I show a lack of integrity.

Let's see how this works. Let's say I don't have a covenantal relationship or agreement with my boss. Then Harry, who works for me, does something unethical. They're Harry's actions, but because I have not been covenantal and responsible, I have tacitly given him permission.

HONEST MEN WHO LACK INTEGRITY

Here is an actual example that happened recently with a client who had committed to become beyond world class. Larry (not his real name) was the CEO of a company who brought us in. He loved the principles and ideas and wanted to start immediately. I led the effort, and Larry spread the word throughout the company.

Immediately, we did what we call a Company Alignment Audit, which is a diagnostic tool to determine the issues we will face. Once we completed the audit, it was clear that Larry either did not understand the depth of the problems he had with misaligned leaders in the company, or else he knew and wanted to fix them.

It became apparent that the solution would not only require a huge amount of work, but also large sacrifices by every employee. In particular, Martin, the COO, would have the most difficult job of transforming the manufacturing component of the company, while we beefed up engineering, design, sales, and management information systems (MIS).

Martin spoke openly about his frustrations with several false starts that Larry had initiated in the past. As soon as they began to impact the "old guard," they would complain to Larry, and soon Martin was spending more time handling politics than directing change.

Maybe this sounds familiar, and it happens in many companies. A leader commits to a cause, but in the middle of the battle he takes the weapons away from his lieutenants.

I met with the officers several times, individually and collectively, to make sure we were in alignment and committed to the correct course of action. Martin continued to doubt Larry's resolve and warned me that once the going got tough, Larry would crumble and resort to the old way of leading by personality and politics, not by covenant.

It took three months before Larry crumbled. I remember having dinner with him the evening before, when I said, "Tomorrow you will have to make a decision. If you want to continue the process, you have to get out of the way and let your leadership team do their work. We know it's the right thing to do. Can you do it?"

Larry looked crushed, but committed to the challenge. I left and returned home to Atlanta.

The next morning, I got the phone call from Martin. As predicted, Larry once again undermined his leaders. Martin quit and so did the CFO—two of Larry's best people and both of them champions.

Larry had good politicians left, but no champions. Within six weeks, Larry's company filed for Chapter 11.

The cost of not supporting champions is far worse than not using them in the first place.

Integrity is alignment, consistent commitment to a course of action, and support for the people who must make it happen. Lack of integrity means we fail to provide the resources needed, or we fail to support champions in the middle of the process, or we undermine their actions because we fear people or we fear to break tradition.

Larry would call himself a man of integrity because he does not lie. He may be truthful, but he is not a man of integrity.

Here's another example from the time I was with a furniture manufacturer. Shortly after I became a vice president of sales, we started a new section as part of the manufacturing division. Because of that, we had to take our wood furniture systems and move everything into a new facility several hundred miles away. We purchased the new facility, and I hired Rick, who had come out of manufacturing, to run it.

Even though I was vice president of sales, Rick came under my authority. I had gone to him and his team and said, "This is what we need, and this is where we are in getting there." In putting it that way, I represented the customers' needs. We faced serious deadlines and it was important to meet the schedule. We were going to shut down production in the old plant in October, and that meant we had to be fully operational in the new plant within days.

We were already promoting our product on more than 250 dealers' floors around the country. "I need your support to meet this schedule," I told Rick and his people.

Rick was trying to revamp the way we made our product. Now that we had an opportunity to start fresh, he felt we could make the items cheaper and yet the finished product would be of a better quality. I admired that because Rick was trying to practice continuous solutions development. He had been sponsored as a champion by his boss, the vice president of manufacturing, and was given the parameters to work within. As he forged ahead, he realized there was one thing he had not been given—the needed resources.

As it came closer to the time deadline, it was obvious that Rick wasn't going to get the new manufacturing system ready. We should have just gone with the old one in place. This new design would carry an initial cost of a million dollars. The simple thing would have been for Rick's boss to say, "Okay, let's just go back and do it the old way." But no, he insisted we would have the new design and that it would fit into the prearranged schedule.

In several meetings with Rick's boss, I had heard him say, "We're going to develop this. And by doing this, we'll reduce cost, increase quality, and ship much quicker."

In a meeting of eight of us vice presidents, the vice president of manufacturing announced, "This is going to cost the company a million dollars." He grumbled about the cost and that we wouldn't have the product within the allotted time frame.

"I feel like firing Rick," he said. For several minutes he belittled Rick in front of the group.

I looked at him and thought, I'm the only other one in this room that knows the truth.

Here was a serious lack of integrity. It wasn't the fault of Rick, the employee. Of course, we could call that a mistake because he hadn't gotten the work done on time—but he probably could have if he had received the resources of people and equipment he needed—resources his boss withheld.

Rick didn't fail. The failure was Rick's boss. Had he been a man of integrity, he would have stood up to the president and said, "I gave Rick the leeway. I told him to go ahead with his idea. I probably should have known better, and told him to do it the old way. But I encouraged him to do it and it's not done."

The vice president of manufacturing was above me at my level and I reported to someone who was equal to him. I sat in that meeting, and although I didn't say anything, I kept thinking what a low-down leader he was—pushing blame on Rick when it was his own fault. I said nothing—and I'm not sure I acted with integrity. My reasoning was that I didn't want to create dissention. The company already had a lot of other issues to deal with, and we would eventually get the right manufacturing system in place.

I left the meeting and went to my boss's office. It was Hal, the one I wrote about in Chapter 12.

"I want to tell you something, and I'm doing it because I'm mad," I said before I even sat down.

"What's going on?" Hal responded.

"I'm going to tell you why I'm so mad. Maybe I'm mad at myself because I should have said something. I just didn't want to create any further problems. But I'm telling you because you're my boss and this situation just isn't right."

I told him what I knew and what I had heard Rick's boss say to him in private. "None of this is Rick's fault," I insisted. "He was led down the primrose path and was promised he'd get engineering and personnel support—which he didn't. He was told there were supplies available and they weren't." I raved on for several minutes about Rick's boss and finally said, "In short, I don't trust him and I have no respect for him."

Hal listened quietly to me. He knew I wouldn't lie to him. When I finished, he pounded his fist and said, "That SOB has no integrity. He's out of here."

Within three months, Rick's boss was gone. Rick stayed.

It's strange for me to relate that story because Hal wasn't always a man of integrity himself, but he recognized the quality in others—and he also recognized when it wasn't there.

I find that most people only see the upside if it works and results in the glorification of the one sponsoring champions. Integrity means maintaining covenantal relationships—regardless of the cost involved. This doesn't center on an individual leading a company, but it means working until integrity permeates the organization. Leaders must first be the models, and integrity is achieved when change becomes evident to the employees.

THE POWER OF MODELS

As I write about guiding principles, I want to make it clear that leaders within a beyond-world-class organization must model these principles. This is important to stress because we rarely see good models anymore.

I can immediately think of three reasons that we don't have models of the kind of behavior that make up strong leaders.

Although I'm now talking primarily about leaders, this works for employees on every level.

1. There Is a Fear of Failure

As soon as we say we will be people of integrity and humility, we set up a very high expectation for our behavior. That brings about a fear of failing. None of us is faultless, so there's no way we'll always be the perfect model for these principles. Our fear then is that if we don't hit it every time, others will call us hypocrites.

Instead, what we need to think is this: As part of the covenant, I will attempt to model leadership qualities as I lead others. In return, others need to allow me to make mistakes. They have to allow me the opportunity to grow—often through failing. That way I'll continue to grow.

2. There Is the Fear of Being a Hypocrite

I need to think of myself as a model *in process*. If I fail 5 percent of the time, that doesn't mean I'm a hypocrite. A hypocrite is one who denies failure or who says, "Hey, I'm perfect," or tries to hide the inevitable failures when they occur. Instead, I continue to say I'm still human, and I need the freedom to be allowed to struggle. Those to whom I model need to expect me to struggle, stumble, and even skin my knees a few times. At the same time, they need to hold me accountable regardless of what happens. As I struggle, I face my weaknesses and I have the courage to fight those weaknesses, because I have the support of others.

3. There Is the Fear of Being Transparent

This means that as we model behavior, we'll allow others to see inside us. It forces us to open up, and that can make us vulnerable. The more vulnerable we are, the more others are able to wound us.

That's the risk side, but we strive for transparency because it's the right thing to do. We may not always get the recognition we deserve. Justice—at least in this life—doesn't always prevail. We still do our best to model what we know is the right thing to do.

In the more than 20 years I've been in business, the best role model I've ever known is J. Smith Lanier. I've never met a more godly, principled man in my life. He doesn't preach to people or point fingers. He's the quiet, faithful model. I've never asked, but I'm sure he has had doubts about his being a role model and been more keenly aware of his failures than his worst critics.

But he has modeled covenantal behavior for me, and I've learned by trying to put my feet in the prints he's left along the way.

If we are afraid to model covenantal behavior—even when we fail—we're also failing those who are walking behind us. We're not leaving clear footprints on the trail for them to follow. As imperfect as our trail may be, at least they'll know we're moving in the right direction and they'll see the direction we're headed.

CHAPTER FOURTEEN

CHARACTER CULTURE
Fairness and Caring

I want to emphasize two often overlooked qualities that we need in the covenantal character. The first is fairness.

Here's a story about fairness involving a union man named Rich. He was a tough negotiator for the union, and he also had offended a couple of influential people in the union.

I was the vice president of a company that had been working on a big deal with the union for eight months, and it included putting several billion dollars into the project. We were all set to announce it.

Rich and I and the others involved in the negotiations reached the union hall just before 5:00 PM. We realized that most of the members had been there since about 3:30. The bar was open and people had been drinking—which was something that just shouldn't have been allowed.

When we arrived, a small group of union people told us to follow them—all of us except Rich—and then took us around the back and down into the basement of the union hall. Once there, we saw the union's executive committee and the shop stewards. It was obvious they had been talking.

With almost no preamble, one of them said, "We've got to talk to you." They wanted me inside alone, and didn't even want to include my team manager. That disturbed me because he's the detail person. I'm the type who puts deals together and depends on others for the particulars. Despite my reservations, I went inside.

"This is what we're going to do," they announced. They were willing to do everything we had agreed on. There was just one catch: "We want Rich gone."

"It seems a little unfair to me what you're trying to do. After all, he's the man we've dealt with and he's the one who has held this thing together. All of my team have confidence in him. He deserves better than this. If Rich had not put this deal together, we would have nothing to offer. He's been your best spokesperson."

"Rich is out," they replied.

No matter what I said, they had made their decision. They dismissed me and rushed upstairs to start the meeting. I followed them—through the back door. That's when I realized that the men had been there nearly two hours and the union leaders had allowed them to drink heavily, which was not appropriate behavior before a major presentation on the company's future.

Two men, who were just about wiped out, sat in the front row. They were already loud, obnoxious, and unruly. They guzzled more beer.

The president of the local union began his speech. He took a lot of credit for the deal—credit that really belonged to Rich.

As he continued, I realized where he was going. He and the others that I had met with in the basement were going to destroy Rich in the public meeting. It took a couple of minutes before I realized that they had orchestrated this thing to do it in front of Rich and that they wanted to humiliate him.

Rich had known nothing of this, although he had been aware of some personal animosity toward him.

I sat at a table on the platform behind the speaker. Rich was near me, so I kept thinking, how do I tell Rich what they're about to do?

Finally, Rich also realized where this was going. He sighed deeply before he leaned over toward me. "I'm okay with all of this. If that's what it takes to get this through."

I said, "Okay."

What they were doing to Rich wasn't fair. He was a man of integrity and had never spoken a word against anyone or demanded credit for the things he had accomplished. He listened in silence while others patted themselves on the back for his work. To the union heads, he became the sacrificial lamb for years of management abuse.

I'm not sure I could have done what Rich did, but he understood that getting the contract through was in the best interest of the union and of our company.

We sat a little bit longer, and somebody from the audience did say, "You know, it's not fair. It was management's fault we got into this trouble."

Those words kept ringing through my ears: *It's not fair.*

Finally, I stood and said, "I've got to tell you something. You'll find out that we will always be fair. Since the day I took over this job, I have always been fair, regardless of how you might feel about the past. What you're doing today is not fair."

"It wasn't fair when they . . ." someone began.

I interjected, "I didn't come here to talk about the past injustices done to you. And they were unfair. I'm here to talk to you about any injustices now and in the future. It's not fair what you're doing. Here's a gentleman that several union leaders have had a disagreement with, but he has been right here all the time, fighting for this union. I believe he is the leader and he's a man I respect." I next explained to them what had happened in the basement and what was going on.

The two drinking men got louder, but I kept talking anyway.

"Let me tell you what would happen if I agreed to what you're doing. We would soon have leadership by popularity. Then we would have leaders who can't lead and followers who won't follow." I stared at the union president and continued, "What you did was not fair. We were set up. You brought me in the back door. You brought my team in the back door. We have worked for months to put this deal together and it's because of Rich that this deal has gotten this far. We will not build a company on a foundation that is unethical, unfair, and uncovenantal. I'm going to leave the stage now and head back to my hotel to wait for your decision. I will not negotiate unfairly, and I will not sacrifice anyone on your behalf.

"I'm going to walk out and I'm going out the front door—the door you should have brought us in through. I want to tell you something. I will always be fair with you in the future. Our company made mistakes in the past and they weren't always fair, but we are fair now and we will continue to be so in the future. If you want to negotiate with us, we do it in fairness to everyone involved."

I walked out of the building, convinced that it was a dead deal. I got into the car and Rich got in and sat down beside me. If this had been a Hollywood movie, they would have stood and cheered as we walked through the center of the crowd. They simply stared.

"You probably blew that deal, you know," Rich said. "You didn't need to do that."

"Yes, I did need to. We're not going to build a company by doing business in the basement. What they did to you wasn't right, and I refuse to be part of it."

We drove to the hotel I was staying at. About 30 minutes later, the union president and two shop stewards came to see me—the same ones who had talked to me in the basement.

"We came to apologize to you," the union president said. He started with the unruly members and the drinking and then apologized for all the minor things. He took a deep sigh and continued, "And we also agree. We weren't fair in the way we acted."

He turned, and for the first time he looked at Rich. "You know we've got some grievances with you, and there are things you've done that we don't like. But we didn't do right by you. We're going to go with the deal."

"Really?" Rich said, the shock evident in his voice.

"We had 479 people cast votes. It was unanimous," he said.

Although I can't identify the people, for obvious reasons, I like to tell that story. When we deal with unions, it's always tough, but one thing I've been aware of is that people want fair play.

This time everyone got just that.

By the way, Rich and I are still friends. I've heard him tell this story and he always adds, "That dumb SOB Alan was going to throw the whole deal away for that."

I know why he likes to tell the story. It's because he was proud to work with an organization with character—one that would not sacrifice principle for expediency or profit.

I wasn't being dumb. I cared. I cared and I was committed to being fair. He thought I would have thrown the whole deal away. What I don't think he understood was that I believed we couldn't build a strong company on wrong principles. If we start wrong, when do we change?

FOUNDATIONS OF FAIRNESS: DISCERNMENT AND WISDOM

Few companies understand fairness; for many, it means simply to settle the conflict. It takes two factors to bring about fairness: (1) discernment—the ability for leaders to see the truth, and (2) wisdom—how the leaders apply that truth.

Employees want to believe that, regardless of the outcome, everything was done fairly. They will even accept a bad outcome if they believe it was a fair one. Coupled with that is the old-fashioned principle often forgotten in most organizations—the art of caring. I believe that leaders need to establish a model of caring that permeates the entire company. Caring then becomes an active principle and allows leaders and followers to put their beliefs into action where many believe it is impossible—in the tyranny of the business world.

In the story about Rich and the labor unions, it's important to point out that everyone, from Rich to the union leaders to the members of my team to the voting members, knew I cared about Rich. I spoke about fairness, which was true. In standing for justice, I also had the opportunity to show that I cared about the underhanded way Rich was being treated.

Caring is difficult to teach. It's a quality that's better modeled than explained. Even so, caring is a vital ingredient in the culture's character.

It's not enough for us to care—people must know we care. As a general rule, when we're concerned about the welfare of others, they know. They also know when we use the words as a veneer or an expression to manipulate.

BEYOND THE EXPECTED

Al Van Kirk runs a company with a deeply rooted philosophy of caring. Kings' Medical has established itself as a beyond-world-class company. It's a company I'd always have liked to work for; however, I'm not sure we would have anything to add.

It is a delight to watch leaders like Al or John Beckett of R. W. Beckett Company and countless others I have met through the years who operate beyond-world-class companies. They have been my models, each teaching in some way the principles you are reading in this book.

For example, the sister of an employee of Al Van Kirk lost everything in a house fire. She was a single mother and was devastated. Through the company's benevolence fund, Al had the staff chaplain reclothe and refurnish that family. Perhaps even more significant, through their financial contributions, many of the company employees participated in the process.

This is an example of active caring. Not only did Al take the initiative, but he also allowed the entire company to share in the experience. That only happens when there is a character culture existing throughout the organization.

CARING THROUGH CRISIS, CONFLICT, AND CHAOS

When does caring move out of the realm of a second-class character trait and into the realm of first class? It may seem harsh to call it second class, but in reality, most leaders see caring as less important than integrity, modeling, or sponsoring champions. After all, these are the traits that transform companies. But caring? The attitude seems to be, "That just makes people feel better."

Too many fail to grasp that caring is at the core of every other trait. How can we truly sponsor others if we don't care about their best interests? How can we be leaders of integrity if we don't care about the people we lead?

Another critical aspect of caring is how important it becomes in times of high stress, especially during chaos or crisis. Caring is at the center of conflict resolution too. It also has a subtlety that the other character traits lack. For instance, when I care for my followers, my attitude and actions inspire caring in them and they can care for me in my times of need.

For years, I had prided myself on caring for my people, my peers, and for the people I came into contact with as I led.

Then I learned something as a person being cared for. At the time I was vice president of sales for the southeastern region of Pennsylvania House Furniture, and I was soon to be promoted.

One day, I received a phone call that my wife Sara, who was eight months pregnant, had been involved in a serious car accident. With her was our three-year-old son Patrick and my mother.

Patrick suffered a concussion and was in and out of consciousness for two days, and they suspected there might be brain damage. My mother had two broken bones. Sara remained at Atlanta's Northside Maternity Emergency Unit; my mother spent two days in their general emergency unit; and Patrick was across the street at Scottish Rite Children's Hospital.

For me, crisis had hit. Despite serious complications, Sara delivered a healthy son, Michael. Patrick had no brain damage, and my mom came to live with us while she recuperated from her injuries. There were no permanent injuries or problems.

While I attended to my family's needs, several positive things happened. The first was that our business didn't miss a beat. The other regional vice presidents took on my administrative duties. My salesforce not only continued with excellence, but they stepped up their performance to allow me the freedom to care for my family. My boss made certain that I had everything I needed.

Besides that, cards and letters of encouragement from employees, our customers, and even from some of our suppliers filled our mailbox, and they were incredibly uplifting. I had never understood the power of caring until I experienced the full force of it in my life.

In telling this, I don't want to ignore the fact that one of the results of the people caring for me in my crisis was their commitment to excellence in the work they do. We actually grew at a time we should have held our ground at best. That's the power of people caring deeply about the needs, hurts, dreams, and passions of those around them. Caring is a beyond-world-class character trait.

I also want to admit that before Sara's accident there had been times when I questioned the benefit of caring about people.

I watched others get ahead when they seemingly "used" people. Sometimes companies passed over great leaders because they weren't political enough or they saw them as too soft because they cared.

Since that experience, I've realized that caring is like a lump of live coal, hidden by the ashes. It takes only a gust of wind to set it aflame. It is energized in crisis and emboldened during times of chaos.

CHAPTER FIFTEEN

IMPLEMENTING BEYOND-WORLD-CLASS PRINCIPLES
Caught Not Taught

For years, I was a leadership junky. Whenever anyone published a book that promised a new approach or offered a fresh revelation on the subject, I had to read it. Most of the time it was like eating the veggie dish at the local Chinese restaurant. At first I felt full, but within hours I was hungry again. For every hour I spent learning about leading, I had to spend countless hours trying to apply the new information in the midst of a world of chaos, pressure, and problems.

My bookshelves were lined with books and the binders from seminars. Too often, the principles never quite made it out of the binder and into business practice. I don't want readers to feel that way about *Beyond World Class*.

We've provided the principles; now, before we return to the tyranny of the urgent at work, here's a plan I've developed for implementing beyond-world-class (BWC) principles.

CATCH IT FIRST

I'll explain how this works by telling about a time when I signed up to be the T-ball coach for Michael, my younger son, when he was little. The teaching-learning process began with tossing the ball. He loved to throw it and then watch it soar through the air. When I told him he had to learn to catch it with his glove, his immediate change in attitude was similar to that of almost anyone trying to apply new principles of leadership.

"Are you ready?" I asked as I prepared to toss the first hard baseball.

"Uh-uh," he replied and shook his head. He held both hands down as if the mere target would be enough for me to throw the ball. "If it hits me, it'll hurt." He was right. That's the same as wrongly applying covenant principles. Our customers, suppliers, or employees use those misapplied principles to abuse us. It can easily happen if we're not prepared. How do we begin to apply BWC principles in a too-busy world and in companies that don't look anything like the model? How do we keep from hurting our careers?

Let's go back to catching a ball. The first time I tossed it to Michael, he held his glove as far away from his face as possible, hoping the ball would drop into it. I aimed for his glove, and the ball actually landed there.

"I caught it! I caught it!" Joyous excitement lit up his face.

We repeated it several times until he grew more confident. If I only had taught him to catch the balls I threw into his glove, he would never have learned to catch. The same is true of us. If we only learn to apply the BWC principles in friendly, safe, and ready-to-accept environments, it is like catching the balls thrown into our glove. But what do we do about the ones we have to reach for, the ones that make us stretch? Learning to apply BWC principles during hard times and in difficult circumstances is like that.

I next taught Michael to move his glove to catch the ball. I tossed it near the glove but not into it. He kept his head and glove as far apart as possible. He missed the ball, as I knew he would, because he used the glove as a shield to protect himself. At other times he twisted his body so much that he faced to the right as his outstretched arm with the dangling glove sought to maximize the margin of safety between the ball and his body.

We do the same as leaders. We try to set the principle apart from the work and the real issues we face. We're afraid of the possibility of failure, because failure means pain, and we want to avoid pain at all costs. I don't want future BWC leaders to experience unnecessary pain as a result of applying these principles. The secret to succeeding without undue discomfort or pain is as simple as learning to catch the ball.

Michael finally got comfortable with the fact that the ball would come to him in a variety of ways, much like the opportunities we have for applying BWC leadership principles. We'll all have the high, hard ones, and we'll also face the slow grounders. Every now and then, an easy lob falls our way. Regardless of how the opportunity presents itself, we need to be prepared to catch the ball.

"Let the ball come to you, son," I had to say many times. "Don't try to protect yourself from it. Use your glove, your arm, and your whole body to get in position. Then let the ball come to you." It took him awhile and he made mistakes, but Michael learned.

As I continue to think of BWC principles, they seem much like Michael's learning experience. If I were coaching you, as I did my son, I'd say, "Let the opportunity for applying these principles come to you. If you learn to recognize the opportunities, you'll learn to position yourself so you can succeed in catching them. If you're constantly out of position, you'll always be running, trying to overcome obstacles that shouldn't even be there. Or worse, you'll run in front of your teammates to catch balls that should be theirs."

LEARNING TO SEE IN THE DARK

Earlier in the book I said that it was possible for BWC principles to be applied at any level of leadership within an organization. It's preferable to start at the top, where leaders model the principles, and then they permeate the organization. That isn't always possible.

When an organization tries to institutionalize the principles, they become just another program handed down from on high that carries little commitment, passion, or energy. In Chapter 19, I will address the source of that commitment and passion that is common in all BWC leaders, but first we have to learn to see the ball and be prepared for the opportunities.

What keeps us from seeing the opportunities to live as BWC leaders? Here are the major ones.

1. There Is No Time to Look for Anything but Answers to the Urgent Demands

Most of us live in the tyranny of the urgent. I wonder how many great ideas and wonderful development plans have been crushed by urgent cries and demands. Consistently, not enough time is what individual leaders and even entire companies give as the major reason for not transforming their culture.

It is an excuse; it is not a reason. All of us have the same amount of time. For some leaders, those hours and days are enough to change the world; for others, those same hours and days aren't enough to finish daily tasks. Time management programs abound to teach us to manage and organize our time. In reality, they usually add more inconsequential chores to already overpacked schedules. Like a lot of others, I've spent much time writing to-do lists. I might have been better off if I had just done something else.

Trying to fit BWC principles into an already overcrowded time management system will *not* work. Instead, we need to do something much more difficult: learn to integrate.

WHEN I, THEN I

I lived through my school years and the early years of my career with the simple motto: "When I, Then I."

- When I graduate from college, then I will begin to apply my skills.

- When I get the promotion, then I will take that course.

- When I finish this project, then I will slow down and spend more time with Sara and the boys.

That principle doesn't work. For us to overcome the tyranny of the urgent, we need to learn to live by a different motto: "While I, I Will."

- While I finish this project, I will find ways to develop solutions to impact the customer.

- While I finish this project, I will apply the covenant skills of leadership and seek ways to bring out the best in all the people I work with.

- While I solve this problem, I will teach my employees how I solved it so they can learn and grow from my experience.

A great part of the integration of these principles into our daily life and work comes simply when we make the commitment to apply them *as* we work. The opportunities abound if we prepare for them, consider the time we have as sufficient, and use that time effectively. Every situation is a potential teaching time, a potential learning time, and the best application time.

As we learn to integrate these principles into our leadership, we see opportunities more clearly than before. As we grow in our ability to see the opportunities, we grow in our ability to impact people; that is, we let the ball come to us.

2. I Work in a Company That Doesn't Care about People, Only about Results

I have heard this excuse often. This excuse assumes that valuing people, creating a culture that adds personal fulfillment, or bringing out the best in others produces fewer results than if we use people to create profits.

Countless examples and extensive research have proven that what creates the best and most profitable long-term results is valuing:

- Excellence

- Creativity

- Customers, suppliers, and employees

- A culture that allows others to contribute, succeed, and attain personal satisfaction

Just because some leaders don't grasp these values doesn't excuse them or give us valid reasons to avoid trying.

Try to imagine this scenario: My CEO walks into my office and says, "People love working for you. Your customers always rate your people and your service the best. Suppliers go the extra mile for you. Your team comes up with the best solutions, and in fact, you've made a huge impact on the whole company. Your contribution to the company sales and profitability is consistently the best. However, I am going to have to let you go. I like the profits, it's just the way you go about your work that I can't stand."

No CEO would say such a ludicrous thing. Yet we behave as if doing the right thing will create the wrong result. Do we need to apologize for accomplishing extraordinary things the right way? We've been conditioned to see weakness in what is really great strength.

One problem we continue to see at CDI is that some leaders do not believe these principles produce bottom-line results. Throughout our careers, we've become conditioned to these lies and that has clouded our thinking when it comes to people values versus money values.

3. We Believe the Three Big Lies of Leadership

Big lie #1: Nice guys finish last. Most of the successful people I meet in business, particularly at the senior level of companies, share a common trait: They're nice people. They're likeable and the kind of people most of us would enjoy a round of golf with.

When we value people, we bring out the best in them, and then they consider us nice people. That's a start. To be beyond world class, we have to do more.

Big lie #2: Always look out for number one. This great lie is based on a measure of truth. Some leaders have popularized and perpetuated the concept of personal success by looking out for their own interests first. The entire libertarian movement popularized by Ayn Rand's rugged individualism personifies this lie, taking it to an even greater level by extolling it as an attribute of human greatness.

The libertarian approach is rooted in the belief that the best way to serve humanity is for all individuals to serve themselves first. On the surface that theory appears to make sense, especially when we consider the rugged individualistic nature of Americans. Ultimately, it's a downward spiral into self-interest and selfishness. In the long run, this approach leads to an "every man for himself" set of guiding principles—and not BWC principles.

There are exceptions, of course, but the best, most successful leaders—and certainly the most highly regarded—all have one thing in common: They forge ahead in their own careers, but they also look out for the needs of others.

There are times when the needs of one are sacrificed for the needs of many. That's why some leaders become great. They're willing to make tough and sometimes unpopular decisions. Even then, they don't sacrifice the needs of many to meet their own self-centered needs.

Big lie #3: I did it my way—and I accomplished it by myself. Much of our culture has been based on the big lie that those who achieve great things do it on their own and without help.

We've been conditioned to believe that nothing matters except achievement—and not the way the results were accomplished. We forget that most lasting accomplishments were done as a result of leaders mobilizing other people in the task. Even those so-called loners had others to help them along the way, even if they don't acknowledge that assistance.

It's all right to admit that we want to accomplish great things in our lives. That's normal and even commendable, and that desire alone doesn't support lie #3.

For instance, when I was a kid, John Wayne was my hero. Even today, I love to watch his movies, even though his incredible screen accomplishments created a myth that some leaders are still trying to live—do it alone and without help.

If we accept everything we see in the films as factual, we believe lie #3. John Wayne's films show us that he did everything, and he did it alone. He freed the Wild West from outlaws, and he single-handedly won World War II in the Pacific with a few hand grenades and a bulldozer.

In reality, when leaders bring out the best in their people—and honor them for their roles—they will show their greatest accomplishments. Those leaders develop a culture of *shared accomplishment*. That's why they're great. They fulfill their own desire to accomplish outstanding feats. As they do that, they also find, develop, and align with the best in others.

4. I Don't Believe That My Efforts Will Make a Difference

Of all the excuses, this one might seem to have the most validity. One committed individual standing in front of the tanks of the Chinese army in Tiananmen Square did not make a difference against the oppressiveness of that regime.

Or did he?

Why is it we remember him? How many of us can forget the picture of that lone student who dared to stand against great odds? We've been inspired by his example and sacrifice.

Throughout history, the sacrifices of one or a few have impacted the world. How many martyrs have set an example for others to follow? During the games of ancient Rome, a zealous, religious hermit named Telemachus could not tolerate watching people being killed by lions as spectators cheered. The vocal protests of this holy man fell on deaf ears. One day, Telemachus raced inside the coliseum and knelt in prayer as the lions rushed toward him.

History records that Telemachus's sacrifice made thousands of people feel shame for their barbarous attitudes. It was the end of human sacrifices for sport in ancient Rome.

LIGHTING THE WAY

Most of the companies I've been involved with have led me to a startling discovery. When I first began applying BWC principles and teaching them to leaders, I believed I needed a culture or environment that would produce results and allow the principles to be effective. I thought that it took an "enlightened" environment for the principles to succeed. I was wrong.

I want to illustrate this point with a story of my childhood. Although I was born in Scotland, I grew up in Canada and all over Great Britain. When I was 14, my cousin Harry and I trekked through the forests and on the beaches of Wales. Near Gelliswick Bay on the Welsh coast, we came upon a deserted and bombed-out fort. Although the posted signs read "Danger" and "Keep Out," we couldn't resist.

"There might be a dungeon," Harry suggested, and that was all we needed.

We could see that it was dark inside, and we didn't have a flashlight. Harry had matches, though, so we made a torch from old cardboard we found near the caves. When we first entered, the torch was adequate, but after several turns, we were deep inside the cave. We frequently encountered small puddles of water that had seeped inside.

After a few minutes, embers fell on Harry's hand. Startled, he screamed and dropped the torch in a puddle. Within seconds, we were plunged into darkness.

THE DARKER THE DARKNESS

I doubt I will ever experience that kind of darkness again. My eyes couldn't adjust in the complete absence of light. When my cousin took out his packet of matches, we realized that we probably needed more than the two he had left. Should we light one and then use the last one to burn the packet?

We couldn't count on anyone rescuing us. In fact, no one knew we had come this way or gone into the caves. Without some kind of illumination, there was no way to retrace our steps. We decided to light one match and race as quickly as we could back the way we had come.

When Harry lit the first match, we made an amazing discovery. The light from that one little match seemed like a giant torch in the blackness of that cave. I remember it vividly to this day. It was as if the light were made brighter by the fact that the darkness was so thick. That single light was enough to point us in the right direction. His second and final match got us far enough that we were able to find our way out.

The point of my story is this: I realized how much of an impact one small, insignificant light can make in the middle of vast darkness.

That is the way it is with beyond-world-class leadership principles. If we have the courage to become that single shining light in the middle of the darkness, everyone will see the light. One leader can make a difference; the darker the environment, the greater the difference.

Even more encouraging is the fact that as we share our light with others—and it will be shared—we'll realize that many lights eventually transform the darkest places into enlightened environments.

Once when I mentioned this, someone asked, "Yes, but isn't it easier when the culture is already accepting of and prepared for BWC principles?"

"Of course," I said. "Yet, isn't it more fulfilling to be one of the first to light the flame? Isn't it exciting to observe one light after another being turned on?"

The fact that we may be the only light shining won't keep us from a commitment to transform the companies we work in. There are probably a larger number of people waiting for us to challenge them—even though they may not be aware of it.

Besides that, even in cultures demanding more of what we do and not how we do it, BWC principles produce the most tangible and long-lasting results. What happens when we let our lights shine?

Well, that's the rest of the story.

CHAPTER SIXTEEN

IMPLEMENTING BEYOND-WORLD-CLASS PRINCIPLES
The Rest of the Story

"**A**nd now, the rest of the story." I love hearing Paul Harvey say those words. His voice is an icon of American radio—and he's the most listened-to broadcaster in the world. His "Rest of the Story" segments are familiar to most of us.

Paul Harvey tells about people who have accomplished extraordinary things, coming from the humblest of beginnings, and then hits us with the punch line. For instance, the lad who toiled tirelessly through school, who seemed to never quite fit in and was laughed at because of his unique features, and who was shunned by many in his own political party was none other than Abraham Lincoln. The approach gives perspective to their accomplishments that we don't get from history lessons.

The same is true of illustrations about companies that have or are achieving beyond-world-class status. When we focus on these companies from the perspective of being successful and then look backward in time, the trials seem less daunting. The difficulties they had to overcome seem almost like part of a script, rather than the potential icebergs that threatened to sink them. When a leader first makes a commitment to beyond world class, she can hope for the same results that others have seen, but she also has to experience the process and potential pain before the results.

When we read about great men and women of the past, we learn of the hardships they had to endure, but we know these hardships are part of the process that leads to accomplishments. We forget that they didn't have our perspective of after-the-fact information to encourage or guide them. Many had little more than hope or faith to keep them going. I've used many illustrations of leaders who have been successful in achieving exactly what I challenge you to attempt. None of them had guarantees, and some of them faced formidable obstacles, but they continued to spread the light.

I want to present an in-depth illustration that best portrays what happens when an entire organization is committed to becoming beyond world class. As powerful and life-changing as these principles can be for individual leaders, when a group of leaders commit at the same time, that's what I call transformation on steroids.

I CAN SEE THE STATUE

Although the majority of this book applies to individual leaders making the decision to impact our circle of influence through these principles, there is a place for an organizational commitment to become beyond world class. I wholeheartedly subscribe to the "one person can make a difference" theory. I am even more certain that collectively we can transform our organizations within months if we apply these principles as an organizational transformation process.

It takes a committed leader at the top or several committed leaders near the top for the process to begin. Thus far, I've talked about and illustrated what beyond-world-class principles are and how they impact the company. Now let's look at how we can apply them throughout a company.

First, I share my belief in the free-enterprise, market-based system that has come to be the standard economic system globally. It is the ideal environment for creating and growing beyond-world-class companies.

In 1953, my grandmother, my mother, my two brothers, and I left Liverpool bound for New York. It was the start of a new life for us and would lead us to many surprising turns along the way. Our father had left months earlier to establish a small hotel and restaurant in New York City.

Dad's arrival at Ellis Island was not what he had expected. After only a few weeks in the city, someone had swindled him out of the entire family savings. The family dream began to resemble a nightmare. For one thing, U.S. immigration laws are quite strict, and because we now had no visible means of support, we were forced to travel to the closest British haven, Canada.

After 12 years of preparation, saving, and sacrifice, Dad was ready to follow his dream again of a family-owned restaurant. This time it would take place in Atlanta instead of New York City. Again, Dad left and we followed. He started his restaurant, but his dream never became reality.

We three sons, now living in the land of opportunity, began to chart our own courses. My brother, Terry, followed Dad's footsteps and became an entrepreneur, and the second eldest brother, Brian, built a fortune through the banking industry.

I'm the third son, and I have felt driven to become the best I can be and to accomplish all the goals I've set for myself.

If we fast-forward 30 years, our parents have died and did not fully realize their American dream, although they pushed us to pursue our education and encouraged us to take advantage of opportunities. Brian became a millionaire and retired when he was 45. Terry has achieved financial success and has tried several times to retire. His love to accomplish things keeps him coming back for more. He works because he chooses to, not because he has to.

I'm the third son and successful in my own way. In fact, all three Ross sons are successful, although we've taken separate paths.

Here's my question: Is it possible that of 23 cousins in our generation all of the success genes pooled only into our side of the family? I think not. We started with one advantage—the ability to apply our lives in a free-market system that rewards entrepreneurs, risk takers, and visionaries. We have been blessed beyond belief to have opportunities that our cousins didn't have.

While my brothers and I don't always share the same belief system, we have benefited from the free-market economy. It is in this environment that beyond-world-class principles flourish best.

That must be why one of my great joys is to see the entrepreneurial spirit energized by the desire to become beyond-world-class. I want to make it clear that I'm not anti big company. There is a spirit of "intrapreneurship" that is just as powerful within larger organizations and, when energized by beyond-world-class principles, makes those organizations a powerful force for change in our society. It takes longer for larger ships to turn around in the high seas, but they still respond to the same leadership at the wheel.

In 1953, we needed to find the freedom and potential to succeed by coming to America. Today, that freedom and potential are flourishing throughout the world. The free market is the market of choice, and even that old bastion of control, communism, has accepted the fact that free markets create the best long-term opportunities for success and fulfillment.

IN THE BEGINNING

In Chapter 7 I shared the application of one beyond-world-class principle—developing customer solutions—that impacted the S.D. Myers Company. The impact of beyond-world-class principles has been far greater there than just the application of this one principle. The company has been transformed forever. It all began with one provocative e-mail that came from Dale Bissonnette:

Subject: Possible Merger

Alan, it looks like the merger will happen. We have committed our joint company to become beyond world class. I'll let you know when we should start. Any ideas?

Dale

Several months later, sitting in the office with CEO Dana Myers and CFO Dale Bissonnette, I explained what the beyond-world-class process would look like, what they should expect, and what level of commitment was needed to become beyond world class throughout the company.

"When do we get started?" Dana asked as soon as I finished.

He and Dale covenanted that day with each other and with my company, CDI. That started the revolution.

Is a covenant all it takes to transform a company into a beyond-world-class company? No, but that's how it begins. The commitment of leaders to adhere to the process and the principles is vital. If they attempt it as another program to get followers to produce more or adapt more quickly, it will be accepted by the employees as just that—another program forced on busy people by a management too distant to understand their real needs.

THE PROCESS OF TRANSFORMATION

I've had the privilege of taking companies through this process. At first, I must admit, I really thought it was unique to me. When I began this book, I realized that I was merely one conduit through which the truth was applied.

If I'm going to leave a legacy, I decided that I wanted to impact far more people and companies than I could touch in my lifetime. I want to be Ramos, the master painter in the modern parable in Chapter 1. I desire to teach these principles and this powerful process so that my one little glowing flame can become a roaring fire that transforms the culture of the world we live in.

If free enterprise becomes synonymous with greed, self-centeredness, and me-my-mine thinking, then it's doomed. Free enterprise must become infused with a higher purpose for it to remain valid; otherwise, we sink into the abyss of selfishness in the guise of success.

Dana Myers and Dale Bissonnette, like others I've previously mentioned—J. Smith Lanier, Gaines Lanier, Jim Nicklas, Dave Lutz, Kent Humphreys, and John Beckett—along with hundreds of CEOs and leaders, were willing to start the process because they believed in the eventual prize. For those of us who are ready, I want to show the process that can transform our world, our company, our department, our team, or even ourselves.

VISION SHARED OR SHARED VISION?

Whether we begin the process in a three-person mailroom or a 10,000-employee company, the first stage is the same. The size and scope of the organization may differ, but the steps to implement change are the same. The biggest differences are the time needed and the depth of application.

The first step may seem easy, but, in fact, it offers the greatest potential for future problems if not taken carefully. For the past ten or so years, the mantra of the business world has been *vision*. Companies paid hundreds of thousands of dollars to firms who helped them craft a vision and mission statement or a statement of purpose. Consultants charged lots of money to wordsmith a set of principles and standards.

In the 1980s, I visited the R.S. Means Company, a well-respected and successful information provider. The company had asked our firm to help them develop a competitive strategic plan because the president, Perry Sells, believed the company had become complacent and vulnerable to competition.

As I conducted the evaluation phase of the process, I found that most of the senior leaders understood very little about their company's vision statement. Posted in large print near the front door, those leaders passed by it every day on the way into their offices. Few of them personalized the content. The former president had paid a consultant to help them draft it. Perry questioned whether it was still valid.

In the executive conference room, the statement was mounted on a large plaque that made it visible to everyone. I read it several times, and although I've long forgotten the language used, I recall that it was wordy and flowery and sounded detached from the everyday work that people did. I removed the vision statement plaque from the wall.

The day came when I shared the process with the senior leadership team of 12 people. After they filed into the executive conference room and were seated, I asked them to keep their hands away from their binders, because they contained small, laminated cards with the vision statement on it.

"Without reading it, what's your vision statement?" I asked.

As amazing as this may sound, not one of them could remember a single statement. I asked them if they could tell me what any of the elements meant.

"We will meet or exceed customer expectations," Perry said.

"What does that mean to me if I am a customer?" I asked.

"It means we will meet or exceed your expectations," someone answered.

"What if my expectations are unreasonable and would violate the value of one of your employees, would you still meet them?" I asked.

"Well, of course not," Perry answered.

"So, you mean you have qualifiers on those expectations then? Who decides what they are?"

No one answered. Even when they grasped some of the components such as "excellence," "highest quality," "leader in the industry," or "high integrity," for the most part, they were just words.

Now, we were ready to move forward. We developed a shared vision, not by spending hours working on the words, but by spending days asking people what they wanted to leave behind at the end of their career. We asked questions such as: "What should a customer expect?" "How should employees be treated?" "What role do suppliers play?"

The first thing we did at S.D. Myers was also the first thing we need to do to change any company—develop alignment to a shared vision that means something to the people we're sharing it with.

Once Dale and Dana said go, we went to the people and asked them what mattered to them. Amazingly, the things they wanted to rally around were some of the principles of the beyond-world-class company.

The S.D. Myers Vision

To lead our industry through commitment to:

Our Customers

- Serve with unconditional excellence in quality products and services.
- Provide exceptional value in creative, innovative solutions to their needs.

Our Employees

- Provide opportunities for growth and personal development.
- Value families and our communities.

Our Suppliers

- Provide opportunities for partnering with us to serve the needs of our customers.
- Provide information and timely feedback to allow them to improve their service while maintaining a competitive price.

What makes these statements different isn't so much what they say but how they were developed. These were the words people had used and were already committed to. This was *their* shared vision, and the words became their guiding principles.

When we ask people what they believe in and what they want to stand for, this is the kind of statement we can produce. People desperately want to work for and support a beyond-world-class company. We need to ask and then let them "own" what we ask them to commit to.

The second step is as critical as the first. Once we finish our evaluations and assessment and craft the vision and guiding principles, the biggest mistake most companies make is the way they communicate this information. Most tend to put the words on a plaque or hand out a preprinted card. These are the *least* effective methods to communicate the information.

S.D. Myers created an environment for change by doing it the beyond-world-class way, that is, the leadership team spent hours deciding what it meant for the company to live this vision and to live by the guiding principles. What would it look like to an employee if we stated we offered "exceptional value"? Could we get away with poor workmanship or shoddy service?

"What does it mean when we say we value families?" they asked each other.

"What does that statement say to the truck driver who is on the road too long and away from his family, because we promised a customer we would deliver on time?"

Every leader had to examine the vision and guiding princi-ples in light of his or her own leadership, because the next step was going to be a huge one. In fact, the real power of the process is found here. Every leader must *personally* share the vision and guiding principles with every direct report. Once they have, leaders were to make a statement that changes the way they will lead forever. They do that by asking their direct reports to hold them *accountable.*

What a switch from the normal process! Usually, we announce that these are the principles we will hold employees accountable to practice. Instead, leaders were asking followers to make *them* accountable.

Most of the time, when we share a vision, we share it with the statement, "This is what we expect of every employee" or "This is what we expect of you." When we change the approach to "This is what you should expect of me," we have energized the process. The onus is then on us as leaders to live by these principles.

We, who are leaders, must be the first to commit.

Dana and Dale made that commitment. So did the entire leadership team at S.D. Myers.

Since Myers had tried many times before to break through to a new level of excellence and profitability, they met with well-earned skepticism. Once the next group of leaders understood this was not merely a cosmetic change but a transformation, they also made their commitments.

They asked every successive level of leadership to hold their bosses accountable, and they were also asked to share these principles with their direct reports. When it reached the final level of the organization where hundreds of workers were asked to hold their own bosses accountable, the transformation really picked up speed.

That's not the end, of course. Just as the S.D. Myers Com-pany experienced, we will be tested. When an existing practice or an old way of doing things stands out in violation of the desired way of doing things, we'll hear about it.

After all, if we tell people to hold us accountable, they will.

Yet, an amazing understanding began to shape the whole company. Soon, every employee was holding each other up to a higher standard of excellence, performance, and profitability. What S.D. Myers was able to accomplish during the final implementation stage of the process was remarkable but not uncommon.

Let's find out what happens when the value of people and the value of profit come together in the right order and for the right reasons.

CHAPTER SEVENTEEN

IMPLEMENTING BEYOND-WORLD-CLASS PRINCIPLES
When It All Comes Together

I could use many examples to illustrate the power of a company-wide transformation process using beyond-world-class principles. I chose S.D. Myers because it embodies all of the aspects of the process in a company that valued people. The founder, Stan Myers, had the most loyal and trustworthy following when he began their transformer oil testing business. To this day, those who worked with him see themselves as part of the family.

Stan's sons Scott and Dana still work in the company, and both live by the principles their father taught them. As CEO, Dana has a large and loyal following, yet something held the company back from maximizing its potential. It wasn't until S.D. Myers had a small but unexpected loss that it began to see the need to change. Although the company remained financially solid, there was a growing sense that it was missing the best and had become satisfied with being just good enough.

D-DAY INVASION

Once the vision and guiding principles were put in place, it was time for the next step, what I call the D-day invasion factor.

When the great generals of World War II planned the strategy for the D-day invasion of Europe, they met in London. All their advisors and counselors sat with them to help make the best decisions and to develop the most successful plan.

The process used to gather vital information and the decisions made as a result of that information became the foundation of success. Using the model of that significant and powerful event in 1944, we developed what we call the D-day invasion factor.

One way to explain this is to respond to a question I often hear: "What makes you different from any other consulting or development firm?"

I don't like it when CDI is called a consulting or a development firm, because we are different. It doesn't matter whether a company uses an outsourced agent like CDI or an internal agent. Both must apply the D-day invasion factor for success. Both must have leaders who are challenged to transform an organization.

As a transformation agent, my responsibility is to help establish the process and assist in the information-gathering stage. We call this the audit process. Many people within the organization can help achieve the best strategic plan.

The difference between a beyond-world-class change agent and other consultants or developers is that we intend to be in the first boats that land on the beaches. In the midst of the battles, we're there to adjust, guide, and suggest. Although transformation leaders cannot actually lead the troops, they can stand alongside the lieutenants and sergeants and support them as they engage the enemy. That's our attitude at CDI: We intend to support our clients as they fight to win the war.

Our involvement isn't a safe, academic pontification 20 miles away from the front lines. We are right where the guns blaze and the bombs fall.

Because of this with-them-in-the-danger-zone factor, we seldom lose an account. The battles sometime rage for weeks, but we're encouraged because we know we're implementing the best plan. That fact makes the effort worthwhile.

I believe so strongly in these principles that I'm personally willing to risk the danger of implementing them. As I pass on these principles, it is my hope that as master painter Ramos did in Chapter 1, I will have taught many other leaders to engage, go deeper, and take greater risks by hopping into the boats with the troops.

If we choose to become transformational beyond-world-class leaders, we can become an internal agent for change within our own companies. If we're head of a company, we can commit the entire organization to this battle plan. We must, however, be sure that those who jump into the boat with us are willing to cross the channel and be ready for combat when we hit the beach.

Sometimes people are afraid that they're alone and can't handle this transformational process by themselves. My experience is that none of us is really alone in this. We may not be aware of them, but every company has transformational leaders. Some are waiting for activation, but they are there. Our task is to spot them, challenge them, prepare them, release them to do their task, and then support them.

TAKING THE STRATEGIC INITIATIVE

Once we establish the vision and guiding principles and gain alignment to them, the next step is to develop strategic initiatives, based on the principles outlined throughout this book.

Here's an example of strategic initiatives that comes from S.D. Myers:

- Develop a Total Account Solutions program to expand our impact with our key customers.

- Restructure the Sales Division to support our Total Account Solutions program.

- Develop and implement a long-term recruitment strategy to seek, hire, and develop the employees we will need to satisfy our growth demands.

- Reduce costs in support areas to increase profitability without reducing services.

- Break down the protective silos—created when departments, divisions, or even offices build walls around each other to guard their own special interests—that have been developed between Production Teams for better use of our plants, equipment, and resources, so that we can serve our customers better.

- Strategic initiatives have the following common elements:
  1. They are specific to an area or cross-functional initiatives that will substantially impact the way the area operates.
  2. They are broad and general with no time limits or specific measures for success.
  3. They align every area to the overall vision of the company.
  4. They force us to think above the tactical and ask "What if?"
  5. They work together to transform an entire organization and to focus on mutual objectives.

How did our own list of strategic initiatives come about? We start by asking the right questions. We focus on the principle of serving customers covenantally. To that we add the principle of continuous solutions development and mix it with a commitment to excellence. We end up with strategic initiatives.

Here is one caveat about the process: Many organizational leaders have been so trained in tactics by focusing on individual battles and not the war itself that they don't readily think strategically. Some are better tacticians than they can ever be strategists. Not every leader needs to be a strategic thinker, but some of them do.

One reason companies employ our services is that we always have to think strategically. If I'm about to get shot as I head up the beach, I want to have a say in where we are going to land. The same will be true of beyond-world-class transformation agents within any company. If we have a great stake in the outcome, we're usually the first to see things from a different perspective.

Once we develop that first set of strategic initiatives, we have just taken the organization through the strategic planning process. From there on, it becomes a matter of learned behavior—a competency of the entire organization rather than something a few leaders do once every few years.

In subsequent years, we refocus on the vision and guiding principles to make sure our organization hasn't lost its alignment.

We ask questions; we conduct extensive surveys. We find out how we are doing from those who hold us accountable. From those answers, we redirect our efforts to anything new that we need to add to our vision or to take advantage of opportunities in our industry or in other parts of the world. At S.D. Myers, the next step was true globalization.

HOW MANY MEN IN THE BOATS?

Once we develop the strategy through strategic initiatives, we connect strategy to tactics and finally to action. We connect beyond-world-class strategy to the action through the development and implementation of vital objectives. Once we know where we're going to land the invasion force, we must decide how many men should be in each boat.

To illustrate, here is a strategic initiative:

Restructure the Sales Division to support our Total
Account Solutions program. Vital objectives in
support of this initiative:

- Recruit one senior sales executive for the Eastern region by July 1.

- Name Bobby Sneed vice president for sales
  and marketing in the Western region and the
  new executive as the vice president for sales
  and marketing in the Eastern division by
  August 1.

- Interview the four current sales managers and
  select two to support the Eastern region vice
  president by August 15.

- Develop a job description, territory maps, and
  sales plans for the eight new positions of Business Development Director. Interview all current salespeople and select those who fit the
  profile by September 1. Recruit and hire any
  additional directors by October 15.

- Reformat the Sales Tech role and interview the
  current sales force for these 32 positions by
  November 15.

- Reduce the cost of travel by 20 percent by
  July 1.

The pattern is probably obvious. These are real vital objectives that came from one strategic initiative.

What do most vital objectives have in common?

- They give legs to the strategic initiative. When they have been accomplished, the strategic initiative becomes an action.

- They are specific, measurable or observable, and time sensitive.

- They are integrated, because each depends on other objectives for the overall initiative to succeed.

- They can be assigned to an individual or team within the functional area of responsibility.

What happens when we put this all together and focus the leadership energy of an entire company on becoming beyond world class?

CHAPTER EIGHTEEN

IMPLEMENTING BEYOND-WORLD-CLASS PRINCIPLES
Sweet Victory

I experience great joy in developing beyond-world-class companies. Of course, we hit obstacles we do not anticipate. No plan is so well thought out that it considers every contingency. If that were true, very few plans would ever make it to the front lines, because things change so rapidly in the business world. There is so much information thrown at us that we must finally make our D-day decision and say: "That's it. The weather is right. The time is right. Let's do it."

At S.D. Myers, we saw remarkable results that give credence to these principles. We have already shared the results of several leaders who applied these principles, but S.D. Myers is the example we can point to for a top-to-bottom transformation to beyond world class.

When the process began, the comment we heard most often was: "We'll just have to wait and see. We've started so many programs in the past, only to abandon the effort as soon as we hit a few bumps in the road. We just don't finish what we start."

What they didn't realize was that once fully implemented, this isn't just another program. Beyond world class is a process.

Within 90 days after we created and implemented the S.D. Myers vision, guiding principles, and six specific short-term strategic initiatives, the process was in full flow. From those strategic initiatives, the senior leadership created 23 vital objectives. As a result, the net return toward profitability was $3.2 million. Given their earlier potential loss, the impact on the company's profit was outstanding. The same leaders, the same problems, and the same opportunities produced incredible results by changing the way they did it. They did it by focusing on beyond-world-class principles.

Even more than the financial returns, what excited me were the comments from senior leaders. They reported that employees were more focused, more apt to support change and development efforts, and more aware of the covenantal way of doing business. Solutions had become the order of the day. Valuing people had become more than a desire—it was now a passion.

In reality, the process of change is just beginning for S.D. Myers. Similar planning and improvements will take place throughout every level of the company long after we have left the scene. I have seen it often enough to recognize that they have passed the point of no return.

As I look back at this success-in-process story, I have to salute Dana Myers, who made the covenantal commitment to start the process. Along the way, he has developed his own leadership skills and is setting the example for others to follow. Dale Bissonnette folded his dream into S.D. Myers, took on his support role with his commitment of a beyond-world-class leader, and continues to model what a transformational leader looks like within a company. Right behind these two are the leaders throughout the company who have passed the flame from one level to the next, until every employee has been impacted.

For example, in one department, a valuable line employee was ready to accept a job offer with another company. Shortly after the process began, he told his boss that he would rather stay at S.D. Myers, because he liked the people and the job. He also expressed concern about its direction and future. After the company began to focus on being beyond world class, he decided the future looked brighter at S.D. Myers and turned down the other offer.

For our CDI team, we feel greatly rewarded when we see a company become increasingly successful because it places its values on higher-order principles. When we have helped to plan and execute the strategy, we see ourselves as part of the victorious force. And victory is sweet! Even better news is that in our victory, nobody loses. That's another uniqueness of beyond-world-class principles.

The only enemies we have to defeat are those within—the ones that allow us to fall into the trap of elevating profit above people. Another enemy is complacency, because it makes us settle for good enough instead of pushing to become our very best.

BEYOND WORLD CLASS—A PROCESS FOR TRANSFORMATION

Whether we want to transform an entire company, a single department, or an office, the process is quite similar. We need to adapt to the size, scope, complexity, and current culture of the organization.

Again, using the S.D. Myers Company as an example:

Phase One: Alignment Audit

Evaluation and assessment of current alignment to:

- Vision
- Mission
- Guiding principles
- Structure
- Competencies
  - Customer

- Internal
- Capacity
- Culture
- Communications

Follower commitment to shared vision

Bobb Biell, who I mentioned earlier, says that if we ask ten people the right questions, we'll learn 80 percent of what we need to know. At CDI, we use a fairly sophisticated approach to conduct a company alignment audit. This includes employee surveys and one-on-one interviews with key leaders. Even so, leaders can approach the change process in similar ways. They do it by preparing employees for change, and the easiest way to start is to ask for employees' opinions. That technique alone is amazingly simple and yet too seldom done in business. (Of course, asking also implies listening and implementing changes.)

If I were the head of a single sales office of a large company and wanted to transform that office on my own by applying beyond-world-class principles, here are ten questions I might use. I'm using these as *sample* questions, because anyone who uses them would obviously have to adapt them to fit their specific situation:

1. What do you believe is the most important purpose for our sales office?

2. How do you think we can align with what the home office expects from us in results? The way we operate? Our commitment to service? Our commitment to excellence?

3. What would you like to see as the guiding principles to serve our customers and support the goals of our company? (They may need to provide examples of guiding principles that would apply.)

4. How well do we serve the best interests of our customers?

5. How effective are we at customer communications? With interoffice communications? With intercompany communications?

6. Are we organized in the most effective way to serve customers?

7. How can all of us improve the way we work together and the way we serve our customers?

8. What are the most important things that you want to get out of your career here?

9. As a leader, how can I better support your personal career growth and your ability to serve our customers?

10. What are our greatest competencies? What are the competencies that our customers buy, our customer competencies? What are our internal competencies?

Each list will be different, but the point is to ask the right questions.

Then listen.

If we establish up front the purpose for our questions, we can allay any fears or concerns.

Phase Two: Shared Vision and Guiding Principles

Develop an organizational vision to include:

- Destination
- Impact on each other
- Impact on customers
- Impact on suppliers or other departments

Determine the guiding principles from employee feedback.

Communicate the vision and principles by asking that you be held accountable to them.

Ask for employee commitment to them.

Somebody has to take all the information and put it into a simple, readable format. Rather than labor over exact words, I suggest using the employees' words. In the S.D. Myers example, most of these statements came directly from employees themselves.

If our company already has a vision or mission statement, we need to include it in ours to have a true alignment. *We then give or add meaning to the original statement as we communicate what it means to live the vision and align with the guiding principles.*

This is also the best place to begin to share the principles of beyond-world-class companies. When we talk with those who do this, they're amazed to find how many employees are ready to get behind the principles.

One word of caution: We can't let the cynics or skeptics deter us. Many people are frustrated and disillusioned in their careers, and if we're not careful, their negativity will impact what we're trying to accomplish. We need to give them time and opportunity to speak. We need to be patient and consistent as we listen. Above all, we need to be their leader. They will change, or they will become so uncomfortable with the culture we are creating, they will opt out.

Several leaders have asked me if they should get their people to memorize the vision and guiding principles. I dislike that approach. Too often it reduces the vision to mere words—like another plaque on the wall, except this time it's in the memory. Instead, I suggest asking people what the words mean. For instance, if the vision contains the statement "We will provide exceptional value to our customers," I would want my employees to be able to tell me what that would mean to a customer. What would be the customer's experience as a result of our living the vision?

We create a much greater depth of understanding when we do it this way.

For small companies, this process helps employees focus on serving customers, while it establishes a foundation for growth and opportunity. When we add statements such as "We will innovate," we set the company up for continuous solutions development. When we add "We will value people," we create an environment where the principles of beyond world class are able to thrive and transform. To say it another way:

- The seeds of change are the principles.

- The soil is the vision and guiding principles.

- The daily implementation and accountability make them grow.

For large companies, quite often we find that there is little alignment with the stated vision or mission. It is not up to individual leaders to ignore or replace them. It is their responsibility to establish the highest degree of alignment possible within the constraints of the company.

When leaders align with a corporate vision, then add value to it through beyond-world-class principles, they have preserved and honored the original and added even greater value to it. I've never seen a situation where an individual leader expanded on the idea of vision and guiding principles, even in one small department, when the company did not affirm the process.

In fact, where there is lack of alignment with an overall corporate vision, the fact that one leader made the attempt to create a greater degree of understanding and alignment was the beginning of change throughout the company. A little light shines very bright in a dark place.

Phase Three: Strategic Initiatives

Conceive general initiatives that will:

- Give meaning to the vision.
- Align to the guiding principles
- Serve customers.
- Develop solutions for increasing customer competency.
- Develop solutions for increasing internal competency.
- Transform the organization.
- Increase productivity, profitability, and performance.

Create interdependence between employees.

Maintain an accomplishment focus (up to three years).

I love strategic thinking. If the vision and guiding principles are the foundation for a beyond-world-class organization, then strategic initiatives become the framework. They provide the outline and format for transformation.

It doesn't take many people to think strategically to get this done, but it will require a few. If all of us lack the ability to think strategically, we need to get outside help from our peers. We can get peer support and perspective from other leaders within our own companies, from contacts at suppliers or trade associations, and even from our customers. We're not limited to our strategic capacity; we can get help wherever we might find it. I imagine that somewhere in our peer groups are good strategic thinkers. Then, we sponsor them as champions to support our efforts. It's amazing how much help peers give if we ask.

The first time I became aware of this willingness to help was when I worked with Bob Frey and Brian Mock at Pennsylvania House Furniture. Many people referred to us as the three amigos, after the characters in a film of the mid-1980s. Others gave us that name because they saw how we interacted and brought out the best in each other. That made us important to the company. Bob was the implementer and the relationship builder, Brian was the tactician, and I was the strategic thinker. They supported me and I supported them.

If we get strategic thinking into our team, these initiatives flow easily. If we try without a strategic thinker, we'll get bogged down in details and minutia.

Phase Four: Vital Objectives

Choose specific, measurable, observable, and time-sensitive actions that will implement the strategic initiatives.

Assign responsibility to one person, with additional support people if needed.

List all the vital objectives needed to accomplish each strategic initiative.

Tactically implement the strategy.

Maintain implementation focus (up to 12 months).

For most leaders, vital objectives represent the place where they are the most comfortable. That is why we spend more time here than in the harder-to-define phases, such as vision and strategic initiatives. It is the vital objective that connects the vision and strategy to the action. It is also during implementation of the vital objectives that we are more likely either to violate or adhere to the guiding principles.

Understanding and communicating the connection between the day-to-day work our followers do and the beyond-world-class principles happens through the accomplishment of these objectives. To continue the D-day metaphor, this is where we land on the beach at a thousand different locations. This is where we begin to win the war. It is also why this phase is the most difficult and dangerous. If we are going to build character, relationships, and profit, it happens at this stage—not in the safety of the London planning rooms. During the implementation of vital objectives is when heroes are made!

Phase Five: Alignment Feedback and Mutual Accountability

Review results.

Adjust methods.

Celebrate successes.

Teach from experience.

Share the beyond-world-class impact.

It's exhilarating to enjoy shared success. Once we have tasted the excitement, we cannot help but spread it. That is why I believe the principles of beyond-world-class leadership can begin anywhere in a company and impact the entire company by virtue of its proven effectiveness.

Increased profitability, productivity, and performance are goals that companies continuously strive for. Valuing people, increasing competency, building character, and developing more meaningful relationships are goals that most employees yearn for. For beyond-world-class leaders, these goals become forever linked, a leadership practice that sets new and higher standards.

CHAPTER NINETEEN

AN UNCOMMON PASSION

In the modern-day parable with which we started the book, I hope you envisioned yourself as a kind of the master painter Ramos. He's like the leaders today who take others to the status of becoming beyond world class. They're the kind who bring out the best—the individual best—in others.

What I also hope you've understood from reading about Ramos is that the best in each of us is unique. No two people are alike. The Ramoses of this life care about, observe, and cultivate the special qualities in others.

Maybe someone has done that for you.

Maybe it's your turn to be a Ramos.

A PASSION FOR PEOPLE

As I conclude this book, I want to point out that every Ramos has one special trait. It's a common factor, regardless of age, temperament, circumstances, or experience. That trait is also remarkably uncommon in the marketplace today.

The best way to explain this quality is to say that it is the fuel that fires a company so that everyone wants to reach beyond-world-class status.

Although the principles I've shared in this book are common elements for becoming a beyond-world-class company, they're actually the results. That is, they are the visible and tangible outcome of the ignited fuel.

I'll use a metaphor to explain this. Several times, I've referred to continuous solutions development and how important it is. Continuous solutions development is the spark igniting the fuel. Exciting challenges, new opportunities, and unique solutions all emanate from the fuel being ignited. The light created dispels the darkness around the flame. Once the sparks ignite, they spread the flames that create even greater light (opportunity) and heat (challenges). Exciting, expanding companies thrive because the flames keep spreading.

To continue this image, covenantal relationships are the flames. As the fire grows, it lights the pathway for others and enables them to walk down the most productive roads. They also have the warmth inside them to nurture their own careers. As their heat increases, they inflame others and stir them into turning to previously unexplored streets.

As the heat intensifies in the workplace and people move down the right path, profits grow as a natural corollary. This happens with the right combination of fuel, ignition, prudent care, and the opportunity that allows the fire to burn.

Profits are *not* the fuel. They are a reason we burn the fuel. If we produce nothing but smoldering logs with intense smoke, but no heat or light, we soon die. I have seen far too many companies that smolder, waiting to die out, but they create just enough smoke and barely enough heat to mess up the lives of the people in them. Fixation on short-term profit has created much of this negative smoke. In the long run, the fuel-produced smoke leaves a wasteland of burned-out people who stare dejectedly at their charred, lifeless dreams.

The true fuel is the uncommon passion that beyond-world-class leaders have for people. These leaders, who are champions themselves, desire the best for others. They impact others so that they too begin to view their work and their life purposes from a different perspective. These champions could measure their own success by the legacy they leave in the lives they touch, the careers they develop, and the champions they sponsor.

Their fuel is passion—and that's a quality like an easily ignited fuel that quickly bursts into flame when ignited or joined with the right opportunities. These champions are passionate for the welfare of people at every level within the organization. Loading dockworkers know a beyond-world-class leader has touched them as readily as the outstanding sales managers. Each person is challenged and encouraged because a beyond-world-class leader takes delight in the growing and contributing person as much as the fruit of their contribution.

This fuel—this uncommon passion—becomes the personal destiny of leaders. They desire their followers to understand and to attain their own goals and objectives. When that happens, they too have realized their own personal destiny.

I also want to point out that leaders leave a legacy of some kind. Just because of our opportunities for leadership, we will leave our marks of influence after we're gone.

What legacy will you leave?

When you walk out of the office door for the last time in your professional life, what kind of heritage remains? On the day of retirement is there a satisfaction within you that enables you to say, "Yes, it was worth it."?

Or will you have to admit your success was measured by profits—additional dollars for the company—with little concern for the people along the way? Will your success be measured by achievers who, in turn, create long-term profitability and do so by walking beside and encouraging others?

A LEGACY OF PASSION

If we consider people as the fuel to ignite profitability, we may be able to sustain some heat and even success in the short run. We may even be able to create one great blast and evoke admiration for our results. But in the long run, the fire will burn out.

Instead of settling for burnout, my major purpose in writing this book is to spread my passion. I want to inflame others so that each of us leaves a powerful human legacy that keeps the flame spreading from one individual to another and from one company to another.

One of the greatest joys in my life is to meet people whom I have led. The best part of that joy is to feel I can honestly share in their success and their contributions to the world long after I have stopped leading them.

That brings me to this final challenge: Is it possible that the greatest reward for a beyond-world-class leader is to see how many other beyond-world-class leaders you can sponsor?

I have used illustrations of many individuals in this book that are beyond-world-class leaders because they all share this uncommon passion. They are leaving a legacy that won't burn out. They didn't do it to be popular, well liked, wealthy, or admired. In fact, most of these leaders had to make many unpopular decisions, but they made them because they were the right and honorable choices. They made hard, covenantal decisions that allowed them to do what was in the best interest of others, even if it hurt them to do so.

Our job as beyond-world-class leaders is to maximize the heat output of the organizations we lead. We have to partially focus on profits, because those profits are part of the heat that runs the economy and that inspires people to take risks, dream big dreams, and reach beyond their current situations. We can expect profit and use that to create more opportunities, better investments, and generous rewards for taking those risks.

Our role is to help people create the sparks that develop into new and bigger opportunities by thinking of solutions. Those who provide solutions are engineers of the future. Without originality, creativity, and ingenuity, we would soon atrophy. Beyond-world-class leaders take great joy in watching their impact start new fires in new places.

We are the leaders who are responsible for creating the steady flame, and who watch and delight in the growth and successes of our followers. That factor of being responsible clearly identifies beyond-world-class leaders. We're not only responsible to promote the flames of passion, but we also can enjoy the success of those we stir up.

This, then, is my challenge to you, as a reader of this book: See yourself as a beyond-world-class leader who identifies seeds of greatness around you. Dedicate your career and your energies toward the principles I've listed. You'll make financial profit along the way, but money doesn't impact lives the way the human spirit does.

The world of business, of government, of education—in fact, every realm of society—seeks for and is ready to follow beyond-world-class leaders. You can be one of those they follow.

I could give you no greater road map to long-term success than the one that begins from within you. As you commit yourself to develop your passion to leave a legacy of unconditional excellence—a passion to make a difference in the workplace and in the world—then you'll become a worthy beyond-world-class leader.

A F T E R W O R D

If I could have met you before you read this book, I would have asked you to commit to three things before you started.

1. I Would Have Asked You to Learn

Beyond-world-class leaders are lifelong learners. They never stop soaking it in, are always curious, and constantly try to grasp new and better methods. They're not afraid to say "I don't know," because immediately after that they add, "Please teach me."

2. I Would Have Asked You to Begin Applying These Principles

I would have asked you to use what you have learned by doing the things beyond-world-class leaders would do. Nothing enhances learning more than applying the principles in everyday, crisis-filled, and chaotic situations.

3. I Would Have Asked You to Teach These Principles

I would urge you to teach these principles to your peers, your followers, and even to your boss. Why don't you become the sponsor of champions by being their master painter Ramos? I find great joy in watching someone I have taught go on and do the job better than I ever did.

I didn't get to meet you. I didn't get to ask your commitment to these three simple requests, so I'm asking you at the end of this book.

Will you commit to them now?

Will you spread the flame throughout your life?

Will you learn the principles of beyond world class?

Will you model and teach beyond-world-class principles?

You have already seen how powerful these principles can be for others. Find out how powerful they can be in your life and throughout your leadership career.

Alan Ross is founder and CEO of the Corporate Development Institute, Inc. (CDI), an organizational transformation and human resource development company. He has served as CEO of FCCI, a large faith-based ministry for business owners and CEOs, and as president and CEO of Design South Furniture. He also provided "turnaround" leadership for several companies during the turbulent late 1980s and early 1990s. Ross served in senior leadership positions at several Fortune 1000 companies before becoming an entrepreneur, and is now a mentor and teacher of entrepreneurs.

Ross is a gifted leader and speaker. Through CDI, he leads a team of high-impact professionals committed to support leaders who desire to create exceptional value while valuing people. CDI has been successful in helping its clients achieve unparalleled success by focusing on the principles and processes presented in *Beyond World Class.* From strategy to leadership development and employee development, CDI is rapidly becoming the leading-edge way of building companies.

In addition to his CDI leadership duties, Ross serves in leadership positions on several nonprofit and corporate boards, and as a speaker for corporate and ministry conferences. His passion for unconditional excellence, valuing people, and creating productive, dynamic companies are hallmarks of the success CDI is enjoying. His personal faith and his wife, Sara, and sons, Patrick and Michael, are his greatest joys and sources of encouragement.

For more information on CDI and its services, contact:

Corporate Development Institute, Inc.
570 Colonial Park Drive, Suite 303
Roswell, GA 30075
770-641-1970

BEYOND WORLD CLASS

For special discounts on 20 or more copies of *Beyond World Class: Building Character, Relationships, and Profit,* please call Dearborn Trade Special Sales at 800-621-9621, extension 4410.

Dearborn™
Trade Publishing
A **Kaplan Professional** Company